Express Lane
Cookbook

Express Lane
Cookbook

Real Meals for
Really Busy People

SARAH FRITSCHNER

ILLUSTRATIONS BY LINGTA KUNG

CHAPTERS PUBLISHING LTD., SHELBURNE, VERMONT 05482

Published by
Chapters Publishing Ltd.
2031 Shelburne Road
Shelburne, Vermont 05482

Library of Congress Cataloging-in-Publication Data
Fritschner, Sarah.
    Express lane cookbook : real food for really busy people / by
Sarah Fritschner.
        p.   cm.
    Includes index.
    ISBN 1-881527-71-9 : $14.95
    1. Quick and easy cookery.   I. Title.
TX833.5.F75 1995
641.5'55—dc20   94-25238

Trade distribution in Canada by: Trade distribution in the U.S. by:
        Firefly Books Ltd.   Firefly Books (U.S.) Inc.
        250 Sparks Avenue   P.O. Box 1338
        Willowdale, Ontario   Ellicott Station
        Canada M2H 2S4   Buffalo, NY 14205

Printed and bound in Canada by Best Book Manufacturers, Inc.
Louiseville, Quebec

Designed by Susan McClellan

To Chris
For Everything

To Nick and Carol
Beacons of Hope at Twilight

The author is donating
part of the proceeds from this book
to provide well-baby checkups
for the infants of teenage mothers.

Contents

· · · · · · · · · · · ·

Introduction

· · · · · · · · · · · · · ·

Most of us don't mind cooking, it's thinking we hate, so instead of trying to plan supper at the end of the day, we reach for the phone—figuring the local pizza parlor knows something we don't—or into the freezer for a TV dinner.

This is dinner?

Perhaps there is a different way, a better way, to get a meal on the table with a minimum of thought.

We all learned in home economics that the best way to avoid thinking during the week is to write down a list of menus before shopping. These menus not only help us plan but also save money. When we go home on Tuesday, we consult the sheet and know what we're having. No need for thinking.

Maybe in my next life I'll have Sunday afternoons free to plot my meals. Right now, I don't have time, and when I do, my plans are just as likely to be thwarted by someone else's agenda as they are to become reality.

Another solution to the dinner dilemma is to shop according to habit. This technique was perfected by my mother, a working woman with

four children who taught me a lot about cooking after work. She was sure she could use hamburger during the week, and flank steak (it was cheaper in the '60s than it is now) and chicken. She could put them in the refrigerator and cook any of them at the last minute when she got home from work.

Main dishes have evolved considerably over the last 30 years, but my mother's theory still operates. We buy more boneless, skinless chicken breast than she did, but we still arrive home and put ourselves on automatic pilot. We open the refrigerator, pull out the food and prepare it the same way we've done it a hundred times before. There's a lot to be said for a weekly repertoire of dependable recipes.

S TUDIES SHOW that a vast number of women (and it is mostly women who make the evening meal) are even less organized, planning their dinner on the way home at the end of the day. They stop by the supermarket and pick up a few things that will—preferably in very little time—become dinner.

This book is for all of us who, despite our best intentions, drive home via the supermarket. But the recipes and menu suggestions are applicable to everyone because even people who love to cook find it difficult to work up a family meal day after day after day.

This, I hope, is the book that will help you make real meals from real food without having to think too much. It is organized for the harried, frantic, time-crunched cook who believes that home-cooked food is better than precooked burgers and fries, but who wonders how there will be time to get the children to school and home again, work, go to a meeting, finish work at home, make dinner and still relax a little.

Using this book, you can prepare dinner (drink and dessert not included) quickly, with nothing more than a trip through the express lane of your supermarket. No shopping for specialty ingredients, no stopping to scratch your head about technique, no pondering what the directions mean. These are simple, straightforward, short recipes designed for family meals at the end of the day, with a minimum of cleanup.

T HIS BOOK HAD ITS ROOTS in a column called "The Express Lane," which I started in the early 1980s when I was assistant food editor of the *Washington Post*. Later, when I moved back to my hometown to become food editor of the *Louisville Courier-Journal*, I continued the column under the name "The Fastlane."

Through the column and now through this book, I communicate with the family cooks who

introduction

have called and written me, pleaded with me at cooking demonstrations, stopped me on the street, talked to me at parties. Each of these people has special circumstances that makes dinner difficult to bring to the table.

These cooks *want* family dinners, think they *ought* to prepare them and want them to be reliable, satisfying and fairly nutritious. The meals can't take a lot of time, and they have to be, if not universally acceptable, at least reasonably pleasing to all the people in the family.

You'll find a variety of techniques and tips for quick dinners throughout this book, in chapter introductions, in recipes and in the little blue boxes. Using just a few of these tips can help you get dinner on the table faster. Begin by making a meal that resembles one you're accustomed to—one that doesn't deviate too much from the cooking you already know. Then you can go on to choose another, and later, another.

Though the abundance of cookbooks in the world implies that we should all have thousands of recipes at our command, in truth we need only a few to be able to provide for our families.

The Dinner Express

WHEN YOU THINK ABOUT COOKING or plan menus, these ideas may help:

● Ask yourself what your family likes to eat and flip to those chapters. I have had countless conversations with parents or spouses who think they ought to be serving or eating a particular food. The fact that your husband *should* eat black-eyed peas, or that you ought to make your children eat salad, are not thoughts that should occupy you when you plan everyday meals. Introduce new dishes when you have not only the time but the mental fortitude to deal with your family's objections. For tonight, spaghetti.

● Plan your meals around acceptable foods. Families eat chicken, they eat pizza, they eat some kinds of soup, they eat most pastas. That's almost a week's worth of meals, if you double up on the chicken and the pasta.

● Practice makes perfect. A repertoire of meals helps the cook in many different

ways. Like learning to ride a bike, cooking is a matter of practice. If you're familiar with the preparation technique, the dish will go faster. Cooking will seem easier and planning meals will require less thinking if you have five or seven recipes you can rely on.

● Identify one or two recipes as your end-of-the-rope meals that you can do with one hand tied behind your back when you're absolutely exhausted. Mine is bean burritos.

● Don't buy into the old models for family meals. June Cleaver may have served meat, potato, a vegetable and bread, but nobody requires that of you. Soup and a roll, or a casserole and carrot sticks, can make a complete dinner. Keep the number of items on the plate to a minimum and you'll keep thinking to a minimum too. Good nutrition is an admirable goal. There are different ways to achieve it: three separate items served in the same meal isn't the only way.

● The simplest things can make a great meal. A piece of chicken coated with flour, seasoned with salt and pepper and sautéed in olive oil requires little effort and no esoteric ingredients. Serve it with cooked rice and broccoli and you have a meal good enough to invite friends over (remember, they'll reciprocate). That's seven ingredients.

● The judicious use of two or three spices, a little soy sauce or some olives goes a long way, adding flavor without effort. Stick a chicken breast in a microwave and you may get a meal, but it's hardly satisfying. Heightening the taste of quickly cooked foods doesn't take special ingredients. A floured and sautéed chicken is delicious with a sprinkling of thyme in the flour.

● There's no magic involved in making dinner quickly, just some commonsense principles. High temperatures cook food faster, so you'll want to sauté, stir-fry, broil and roast on high heat more often than you bake at 350 degrees or braise or simmer. Cutting food into small pieces helps speed cooking, though you may need to invest more time at the beginning. Large skillets accommodate more food than small ones, cutting down on the cleanup; they also allow liquid to evaporate quickly and the food to cook faster.

● Get yourself a sharp knife. If you love cooking, you'll love it more with a good knife. If you hate cooking, a good knife will change your life. You'll be able to prepare food faster and easier, and you'll drastically reduce the time you spend in the kitchen.

Soups

SOUPS HAVE A REPUTATION as long-simmered affairs, bubbling away on the stoves of people who have time to make rich broths and chop endless amounts of vegetables. These hearty combinations take their place prominently in our imaginations, not on our menus.

But not all soups require huge beef bones, multistep browning, time-consuming simmering and labor-intensive chopping. In fact, some homemade soups can be lifesavers for busy cooks who haven't had time to plan dinner.

In former times, people made soup stock from animal bones because they had both the bones and the time to simmer them. These days, nobody has time, and boneless chicken breast has become a lot easier to find than beef knuckle bone. Luckily, however, good soup can be made from canned broth or bottled clam juice and tomato juice, or a combination of the two. Canned broths have greatly improved, and though they may not duplicate the stock made from an aged hen simmered most of the day on the back of a wood-burning stove, they substitute admirably when the cook has only 30 minutes to make dinner.

Other convenience products come to the rescue in making quick soups. It takes seconds to cut boneless chicken breast into chunks and just moments to simmer it.

Aged and smoked meats like bacon, sausage and ham add tons of flavor and are effortless additions. A little goes a long way, so you don't have to worry about the fat. Often I'll cook three pieces of bacon until crisp, then add them along with vegetables to the pot.

Crushed tomatoes in a can and frozen vegetables are also remarkable timesavers when it comes to making soup. If you want to add a fresh taste, use these products in tandem with sautéed onion and garlic.

Some traditional soup recipes need no tinkering with, for they require few ingredients and short cooking time—with no apologies made. Fish chowders, for instance, rely on milk (or cream), onions, potatoes and fish, which would be ruined if overcooked.

These can be ready in minutes.

IN ADDITION TO THEIR CONVENIENCE, soups often make vegetables more appealing. For the child who won't eat spinach, cream of spinach soup is a delicious camouflage. Minestrone incorporates beans, vegetables and pasta. Lima beans in chicken vegetable soup are palatable to children who won't abide them alone on the plate.

Remember, too, that adding pureed vegetables, beans and rice imparts creaminess to soups. So the next time you make "cream of broccoli," consider using potatoes or rice as the thickener. Puree in a blender, which works better than a food processor, and you'll get plenty of body but far less of the fat and calories you'd get with cream. You won't believe how silky sweet potatoes can be until you've pureed them in soup (add a little jalapeño pepper for bite). Then stir in milk, or nonfat milk powder, if you prefer.

With thin brothy soups, serve a substantial side dish—green chile corn bread (page 186) or even a sandwich. For heartier gumbos and bean soups, a simple garnish may be all you need. Grated cheese, a dollop of sour cream or a few croutons top things off nicely.

soups

Magic Croutons

· ·

CROUTONS ADD ELEGANCE TO SOUP AND SALAD, yet they are easy and inexpensive to make.

Start with leftover bread of any kind. French baguettes are good; my brother even uses leftover hot dog buns. Any type of bread will work.

To toast French-bread croutons: Preheat the oven to 400 degrees.

Cut the loaf into slices about ½ inch thick, spread with butter or drizzle with olive oil and toast in the oven for 10 minutes, or until brown and crunchy. Sprinkle with cheese before toasting to make them extra savory.

Whole slices of French bread can be used in the bottom of a bowl before the soup is ladled in (as is traditional with onion soup), placed on top of soup or served to the side of a mixed-green salad.

To make cubed croutons: Preheat the oven to 350 degrees.

Cut any leftover bread (including whole wheat, rye and cheese breads) into ½- or 1-inch cubes and sprinkle with olive oil.

Bake in the oven until crisp. Use to top soups or salads. Store extra croutons in the refrigerator or freezer.

Broccoli Cheese Soup

· ·

Broccoli and its cousins (cauliflower, Brussels sprouts and cabbage) contain one of the most powerful anticancer agents ever discovered. Broccoli also is rich in fiber and vitamin A, two other cancer fighters. But that doesn't do us any good unless we eat it. One delicious way to prepare broccoli is in Broccoli Cheese Soup. A thrifty cook will make this with broccoli stems. A hurried one will make it with frozen broccoli pieces: it's delicious either way.

1	14-to-16-ounce can (about 2 cups) chicken broth
3	cups chopped broccoli (from 1 medium head; stems are fine)
½	cup chopped celery
2	tablespoons butter or margarine
4	tablespoons all-purpose flour
½	teaspoon salt
	Freshly ground pepper
4	cups milk (skim is fine)
½-1	cup grated aged Cheddar
4	broccoli florets (optional)

In a medium saucepan, bring broth, broccoli and celery to a boil over high heat. Reduce heat to medium and simmer until broccoli is tender (smaller broccoli chunks will cook faster than larger ones), about 5 to 10 minutes. Stir once or twice.

If you want a smooth soup, puree broccoli in a blender.

Meanwhile, melt butter or margarine in a large saucepan over medium heat. Stir in flour, salt and pepper to taste; cook for 1 minute. With a whisk or a wooden spoon, add milk gradually, beating constantly to prevent lumping. (It will thicken like paste at first; keep beating in milk to thin it.)

Bring to a boil and add broccoli and its liquid, either pureed or in chunks.

Remove from heat and stir in cheese. Ladle into individual bowls and garnish with broccoli florets, if desired.

Serves 4. ∽ **Serve with ham sandwiches.**

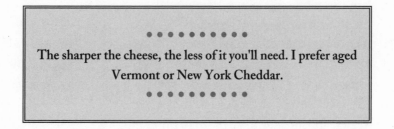

• • • • • • • • • •

The sharper the cheese, the less of it you'll need. I prefer aged Vermont or New York Cheddar.

• • • • • • • • • •

Cream of Broccoli Soup

· ·

COOKED POTATO ADDS CREAMINESS to this soup, cutting down on fat, calories and steps.

2   tablespoons butter or vegetable oil
1   medium onion, sliced
1   large head broccoli (about 1½ pounds), trimmed, tough stems peeled
1   large potato (no need to peel)
2   14-to-16-ounce cans (about 4 cups) chicken broth
    Salt and ½ teaspoon freshly ground pepper
    Water, milk or additional broth to thin soup, if needed
    Magic Croutons (page 17, optional)
2   ounces blue or Roquefort cheese (optional)

· · ·

You can add chunks of cooked chicken to this soup to make it more substantial.

· · ·

Heat butter or oil in a large pot over medium-high heat. Add onion and cook until soft, about 10 minutes.

Cut broccoli stems into small chunks and broccoli head into florets. Cut potato into small chunks. Set aside 4 broccoli florets.

Add remaining broccoli and potato to the pot, along with chicken broth. Season with salt and pepper. Simmer for 20 minutes, or until broccoli and potato are tender.

Transfer contents of pot, one-third at a time, to a blender. Blend until smooth. Return to the pot; bring to a boil. Thin soup with water, milk or broth.

Serve in hot bowls, topped with a broccoli floret or croutons and crumbled blue cheese, if using.

Serves 4.   ∾   Serve with turkey sandwiches.

Creamy Spinach Soup

CREAM SOUPS NEEDN'T BE FATTENING or difficult. If you have a blender or a food processor (a blender works best), you don't need cream or even a mixture of butter and flour to make a smooth soup. In reduced-fat creamy soups, blended vegetables or starches add body without a lot of calories.

Horseradish perks up this spinach soup, which is super-easy because it's made all in one pot.

2   medium potatoes, unpeeled and chopped
1   cup water
1   10-ounce package frozen chopped spinach
1-2 teaspoons prepared horseradish
     Salt, freshly ground pepper and nutmeg
       to taste
3   cups milk
½-¾ cup grated Swiss cheese (optional)
     Sour cream for topping (optional)

• • •

When you have
finished with the
blender, make cleanup
easy by blending hot
soapy water in it,
then rinsing.

• • •

Place potatoes in a large saucepan with water. Simmer over medium heat for about 10 minutes. Add spinach, horseradish, salt, pepper and nutmeg. Simmer for 10 minutes more, or until potatoes are tender and spinach is thawed.

Pour into a blender and blend until smooth, adding milk gradually. Return to the pan and simmer until heated through, stirring occasionally. Serve, topped with a little grated cheese and/or sour cream, if using.

Serves 4. ～ Serve with chicken sandwiches (page 87).

Curried Pea Soup

• • • • • • • • • • • • • • • • • • •

PEAS ARE LITTLE POWERHOUSES OF NUTRITION. A cup of peas has twice the iron, more protein and only 30 more calories than an egg. Better still, while an egg has nearly 6 grams of fat, a cup of peas has only ½ gram.

This pea soup is as quick as it gets. Notice that it doesn't even require peeling the potato—everything gets blended in the end. The "creaminess" comes from the peas and potatoes. Once they're pureed, they'll make a thick soup. To make it vegetarian, substitute water for the chicken broth and add a handful of fresh, minced parsley before blending.

2 cups frozen peas or one 10-ounce package
1 medium onion, chopped
1 small carrot, chopped
1 celery rib, trimmed and chopped
1 medium potato, unpeeled, chopped
½ teaspoon salt, or more to taste
2 teaspoons curry powder
1 14-to-16-ounce can (about 2 cups) chicken broth
2 cups milk

Combine vegetables, seasonings and 1 cup broth in a medium-size saucepan; bring to a boil over medium-high heat. Cover and reduce to medium. Simmer for 15 minutes, or until vegetables are tender.

Transfer mixture to a blender and blend until smooth. Add remaining 1 cup broth while the blender whirs. Return soup to the pan and stir in milk. Simmer until heated through, stirring occasionally.

Pour into warm bowls.

Serves 4. ∾ Serve with cheese toasts or tuna sandwiches.

Spaghetti Soup

• • • • • • • • • • • • • • •

CONVINCING PEOPLE TO EAT FOOD THAT'S GOOD for them takes some marketing skill. One friend got her third-grader to try lentil soup by floating a few disks of hot dog on top and calling it "hot dog soup." Children may be more excited about this quick vegetable soup if you call it spaghetti soup. You can also add an ounce or two of diced pepperoni to the onion and spaghetti and call it "pizza soup."

3 tablespoons vegetable oil
⅔ cup broken (1-inch lengths) thin spaghetti
½ medium onion, chopped
2 garlic cloves, minced
1 16-ounce can garbanzo beans (chickpeas)
1 15-ounce can stewed tomatoes, broken up
1 10-ounce package frozen mixed vegetables
1 14-to-16-ounce can (about 2 cups)
    chicken broth
2 cups water
2 teaspoons Italian herb seasoning
  Salt and freshly ground pepper to taste
  Parmesan cheese to taste

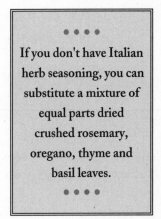

• • • •

If you don't have Italian herb seasoning, you can substitute a mixture of equal parts dried crushed rosemary, oregano, thyme and basil leaves.

• • • •

Heat oil in a large saucepan over medium-high heat. Add spaghetti and onion to the pan and sauté for 2 to 3 minutes; add garlic. Reduce the heat to medium and cook until onion is translucent.

Add remaining ingredients, except Parmesan. Bring to a boil, reduce heat to low and simmer for 10 minutes until heated through.

Sprinkle with Parmesan cheese and serve.

Serves 4.   ∾   Serve with chicken or tuna sandwiches.

Easy Tomato Bisque

• •

MY SISTER-IN-LAW DOESN'T LIKE TO COOK. Unfortunately, she's surrounded by people who do, so the pressure is intense. She has perfected a few great dishes. The following tomato soup is one of them; she serves it cold in the summer. Is this soup wonderful because it's so easy? The unexpected seasoning of cloves adds a mysterious dimension.

1	quart home-canned tomatoes or one 28-ounce can
1	large onion, chopped
5	whole cloves
2	bay leaves
1½	teaspoons sugar
	Salt and freshly ground pepper to taste
4	tablespoons plain yogurt or sour cream

Combine tomatoes, onion, cloves, bay leaves, sugar, salt and pepper in a medium-size saucepan. Simmer over medium-high heat until onions are tender, about 15 minutes. Remove cloves and bay leaves.

In two batches, whir in a blender until smooth. Return to the saucepan, simmer until heated through, and season to taste.

Serve hot or cold, topped with yogurt or sour cream.

Serves 4. ∾ Serve with tuna melts (tuna salad topped with a slice of melted cheese) on English muffin halves or a grilled roast beef sandwich.

Mexican Holiday Soup

T HERE ARE SOME NIGHTS WHEN OPENING A CAN is about all I'm able to handle. This soup was made for that kind of evening. Its clean vegetable taste has a little bite from the green chilies— nothing remotely hot. I like to serve it during the holidays, when I need a break from rich food.

You can also make it in summer. If you have fresh garden vegetables, use them.

1   tablespoon olive oil or vegetable oil
1   medium onion, chopped
2   garlic cloves, chopped
1   28-ounce can tomatoes
2   10-ounce packages frozen corn
1   4-ounce can chopped mild green chilies
1   chicken breast half, cut into small chunks
1   14-to-16-ounce can (about 2 cups) chicken
        broth
2   cups water
1   teaspoon dried oregano
    Salt to taste

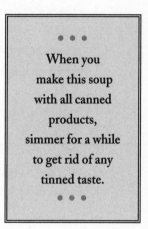

When you make this soup with all canned products, simmer for a while to get rid of any tinned taste.

Heat oil in a large saucepan over medium-high heat. Add onion and garlic and sauté until translucent, about 10 minutes.

Drain liquid from tomatoes into the saucepan and chop tomatoes well. Add tomatoes to the pan with remaining ingredients. Reduce heat to medium and simmer until heated through, stirring occasionally. Season with salt, if desired.

Serves 4 to 6.   ～   Serve with corn bread (page 186) or grilled cheese sandwiches.

Quick Chicken and Rice Soup

· ·

THIS SOUP IS CHUNKIER AND FRESHER TASTING than the canned version I loved when I was a child. Simmered with the herbs and vegetables, it begins to taste as if it took all day to make.

3	14-to-16-ounce cans (about 6 cups) chicken broth
5	cups water
½	cup raw long-grain white rice or brown rice
2	carrots, trimmed and diced
2	celery ribs, trimmed and diced (include leaves)
1	medium onion, diced
1	teaspoon salt
1	teaspoon dried thyme
¼	teaspoon freshly ground pepper
4	boneless, skinless chicken breast halves

Combine all ingredients except chicken in a large saucepan or Dutch oven. Bring to a boil over high heat, reduce heat to medium and simmer for 20 to 40 minutes (20 for white rice, 40 for brown), or until rice is tender.

Meanwhile, slice chicken into small chunks and add to soup 5 minutes before rice is cooked.

Serves 6 generously. ∽ **Serve with hot biscuits (page 180) and carrot sticks.**

Variations

Budget Chicken Soup: Use a whole, cut-up chicken or all dark meat as a substitute for expensive boned chicken breast. Remove all skin and fat from the chicken pieces. If using white and dark meat, add the dark meat to the broth first so it has more time to cook. About 5 minutes before the soup is done, remove the chicken pieces with a slotted spoon. Pull the meat off of the bones, discard the bones, chop the meat and return it to the soup.

Quick Chicken Noodle Soup: Omit the rice and simmer for 20 minutes; substitute noodles. Noodles should cook for about 8 minutes, or until very tender.

Plenty Hot Chili

· ·

CHILI MAKES A WONDERFUL SUNDAY AFTERNOON PROJECT. Unfortunately, many of us don't have long afternoons to devote to cooking. If you love chili, but hate to spend hours in the kitchen, try this recipe.

Adding cornmeal to the pot not only thickens the broth, it gives a wonderful flavor and texture to the mixture.

2	tablespoons vegetable oil
2	medium onions, minced
5	garlic cloves, minced
3	pounds lean ground beef
3	14-to-16-ounce cans (about 6 cups) beef broth
1	cup water
¼	cup chili powder, or less to taste
1	tablespoon ground cumin
1	tablespoon dried oregano
1½	teaspoons cayenne pepper (optional)
1	teaspoon salt
3	tablespoons cornmeal

· · ·

Know thy chili powder. In some parts of the country, it is ultramild. In other places, half this amount will be hot. Start with 2 tablespoons and work from there.

· · ·

Heat oil over medium-high heat in a large Dutch oven. Add onions and garlic and cook for 10 to 15 minutes, stirring occasionally to prevent burning, until transparent. Scrape onion mixture into a bowl and set aside.

In the same pot, brown beef, stirring occasionally to break up clumps. Drain all fat; add onion mixture, beef broth, water, chili powder, cumin, oregano, cayenne pepper, if desired, and salt.

Bring to a boil over high heat, reduce heat to medium and simmer for 15 minutes to blend flavors.

Sprinkle in cornmeal; stir well to blend. Simmer for 10 minutes more to thicken the mixture.

Serves 6 to 8 generously. ∽ **Serve with saltines and sliced tomatoes or with pinto beans and fresh fruit.**

Quick Chili

• • • • • • • • • •

THIS CHILI REQUIRES NO TALENT TO COOK. If you can brown hamburger and open cans, this is the recipe for you. In the South and Midwest, cooks are known to add spaghetti to their chili, and I usually do to this one. The chili improves if you cook it for a while. Let it simmer for 15 minutes, and the spices will help mellow the tinny flavor.

If your family likes spicy chili, you may want to add cayenne pepper with the other spices, and serve pickled jalapeño peppers on the side.

1	pound lean ground beef
2	tablespoons olive oil or vegetable oil
3-5	garlic cloves, minced
1	teaspoon ground cumin
1	teaspoon chili powder
1	teaspoon dried oregano
1	16-ounce can pinto beans (about 2 cups cooked)
1	4-ounce can chopped mild green chilies
1	28-ounce can tomatoes
	Salt and freshly ground pepper

> • • •
>
> Double the recipe and serve as chili. Freeze the leftovers, and the following week, combine them with salsa and fill tortillas with the mixture for burritos.
>
> • • •

Brown ground beef in a large Dutch oven over medium-high heat, stirring occasionally to break up clumps. When it is brown all over, remove with a slotted spoon and drain on a paper towel set on top of a paper bag. Discard excess fat from the pot.

Add oil and garlic and cook over medium-high heat until the garlic is golden, about 2 to 5 minutes, stirring occasionally to prevent burning. Add cumin, chili powder and oregano; stir for 1 minute to coat garlic with spices.

Add cooked beef, beans, chilies and tomatoes, chopping tomatoes as you add them (the less time you have to cook tomatoes, the smaller you should cut them).

Heat through or simmer for at least 15 minutes. Season with salt and pepper to taste.

Serves 6 generously. ∾ **Serve with saltines or over boiled spaghetti, if desired, and/or topped with cheese, with carrot sticks and/or apple slices on the side.**

Variations

Beanless Budget Chili: If the people in your family refuse to eat beans, you can add bulgur (cracked wheat) to the chili. Add 1 cup bulgur and 2 cups water, beef broth or tomato juice with the ground beef and tomatoes.

Beef and Bean Burritos: Lightly grease a 9-by-13-inch casserole dish. Spread ½ cup salsa in the bottom of the dish. Place ¼ cup chili in corn or whole wheat tortillas and top with 2 tablespoons grated Cheddar; roll up tortillas. Place filled tortillas in the dish, seam side down. Top with grated Cheddar and bake at 350 degrees for 20 minutes, or until cheese is melted and burritos are heated through. Serve with extra hot salsa, if desired.

Salads

• • • • • • • • • • • • •

AMERICAN COOKS generally think of one thing as a salad: lettuce, as often as not iceberg. While iceberg lettuce *is* quick when you're rushed—it doesn't need to be painstakingly washed to remove grit and then crisped—it isn't the best-tasting variety. That might be OK if it had some redeeming nutritional value. It doesn't.

Like restaurant chefs, we need to expand our definition of salads and realize that they don't have to consist of lettuce. This is good news for the busy cook who may not have time at the end of a day to wash lettuce leaves, prepare salad accoutrements and the other necessary chores a leaf-lettuce salad demands. On most nights, my family would go saladless if I depended on lettuce.

And like chefs, we also need to practice marketing. In restaurants, raw carrots aren't carrot sticks, they're crudités. That's kru-dee-TAY: French for "This is salad, buster."

We can take inspiration from gourmet

carry-outs, which make their fortunes on nonlettuce salads. Chunky fruit salads or vegetable salads are great keepers: they can sit for one day, or even two, without wilting the way leaf lettuces would. In fact, many of these vegetable salads actually improve in the refrigerator over time: they're marinating, not declining.

AT OUR HOUSE, broccoli salad is a favorite: blanched broccoli with a simple vinaigrette and perhaps some chopped red bell pepper and/or chopped olives. You can smush an anchovy in the dressing and call it "Broccoli Caesar."

Coleslaw, that great standby, also gets better as it sits. Vary it with different mixtures of cabbage (purple, green, Chinese, Savoy) and by adding shredded or julienned vegetables: green pepper, carrot, radishes . . . whatever you like.

Three-bean salad is another favorite, in part because it, too, improves over time. Substitute black beans, corn and bell pepper for the usual beans or just make a big bowl of marinated green beans. They'll keep for a week in the refrigerator.

REMEMBER THAT COOKED VEGETABLES from tonight can become salad for tomorrow. Dress leftovers and chill them for the next night.

Let the seasons be your guide. Consider what's cheap at the supermarket. Lettuce has its seasons, but the height of summer isn't one of them. Summer salads can be made at the last minute from sliced tomatoes or cherry tomatoes tossed with herbs. In winter, sliced oranges and/or grapefruit and maybe an avocado dressed with vinaigrette become a refreshing salad.

When you're really in a rush, shop at the supermarket salad bar, where the vegetables have already been prepared by someone else. For the best bargains, choose lightweight items like lettuce and sliced mushrooms, and add your own dressing and hard-boiled eggs later. Fresh spinach is a good buy because you get a lot for your money, it's vitamin-rich, and it has already been through the labor-intensive stemming and multiple washings.

Whether dinner is a broiled chicken breast, a grilled steak, a Reuben sandwich or a bowl of chili, a salad is nearly always a perfect side dish.

The Perfect Tossed Salad

. . . .

THE PERFECT TOSSED SALAD REQUIRES TWO THINGS: good lettuce and a good dressing. Everything else is optional.

There are several ways to fulfill these requirements, but supermarket leaf lettuce and a home-made oil-and-vinegar dressing are a perfect pair—simple yet dignified, even if they aren't exotic.

To make the perfect lettuce salad, follow these suggestions:

● Use leaf lettuce, such as romaine, Boston or Bibb. They offer better flavor, texture and more nutrition than iceberg lettuce. The darker the leaves, the higher the vitamin A content.

● To prepare leaves ahead of time, wash well and shake dry. Wrap loosely but completely in a cloth or paper towel. Insert the bundle into a plastic bag. Store in the refrigerator. Romaine leaves are especially durable—they will last for several days in the refrigerator.

This wrapping and chilling treatment will usually dry your lettuce leaves. Lettuce leaves should be completely dry to make a good salad: the dressing clings to the leaves instead of dropping to the bottom of the bowl.

● There are other ways to dry your salad leaves: you can use clean cloth towels (or the less eco-friendly paper) and pat them dry.

Though I'm not much on gadgets, a salad spinner is one I depend on. It's available at cookware stores, and I've often seen them in old-fashioned neighborhood hardware stores too. Spinners dry leaves completely and aren't laborious to clean because nothing sticks to them: a quick rinse will usually do the trick. The bowl of the spinner can be used to store clean lettuce leaves for tomorrow night, another plus.

Optional Extras

● Add something salty to a salad. Olives and anchovies are a special touch. If you have them (and like them), use just a little, say 2 tablespoons of minced olives in a salad for 4.

● Add something rich. Croutons, cheese or nuts, in small amounts, enhance any salad. Walnuts, sunflower seeds, pecans, cashews and pine nuts can make the salad special. Toast them first, if you have time. Toasting brings out the flavor like you won't believe. Nuts may be toasted in a dry skillet on top of the stove or in the oven. The slower you toast them, the more evenly they brown and the less likely they are to burn. If you do it in a skillet, stir often and keep the heat pretty low (or turn the heat higher and stir constantly, removing the skillet from the flame occasionally to moderate the heat). Or you can spread the seeds on a cookie sheet and toast them in the oven at 350 degrees. Stir occasionally so they brown evenly; if you don't stir, the seeds on the outside will brown much faster than the seeds in the middle.

● Other added attractions: Overloading a lettuce salad with raw cauliflower or carrots does not always make it taste better. But a little can be delicious. Ditto for ham, tomatoes and hard-boiled egg.

● Fresh herbs can add a mysteriously delicious quality. If you grow fresh herbs (and I recommend you do; it's easy), add 1 or 2 tablespoons of leaves to the salad.

Great Vinaigrette

· · · · · · · · · · · · · · · · · · · ·

THERE ARE LOTS OF THEORIES ON VINAIGRETTES: 1 part vinegar to 3 parts oil, 4 parts oil or even 5 parts oil. Some cooks subscribe to the unusual-nut-oil school of vinaigrette and make their dressing with walnut or hazelnut oil. Others think that vinegar has to travel at least 3,000 miles to reach perfection and make their dressings with sherry vinegar or balsamic vinegar.

My advice: don't be obsessive. This dressing is good when made with the moderately priced olive oil, wine vinegar and European-style mustards you can find in nearly any supermarket. But by all means, if all you have on hand are apple cider vinegar and German mustard, use them. If you want blue-cheese dressing, add blue cheese to the lettuce and top with the oil-and-vinegar mixture.

This vinaigrette takes little time to make and stores well in the refrigerator.

¼ cup olive oil or vegetable oil
1 tablespoon vinegar (any type)
1 teaspoon Dijon-style mustard or other
  European-type mustard
½ teaspoon salt
  Freshly ground pepper to taste

· · ·

You can also use this mixture to marinate meat for grilling or broiling.

· · ·

Combine all ingredients in a jar. Close the lid tightly and shake to blend. Taste and add more salt, if necessary.

Makes about ⅓ cup.

Mustard Vinaigrette

. . . .

THIS DRESSING IS JUST A LITTLE SHARPER than the one in the preceding recipe, with a little more vinegar and a slightly higher proportion of mustard. Also, it contains garlic, which I love.

1	garlic clove, minced
3	tablespoons red or white wine vinegar
2	teaspoons Dijon-style or other spicy mustard
¼	teaspoon salt
¼	teaspoon freshly ground pepper
⅓-½	cup olive oil or vegetable oil

In a small jar or blender, shake or blend all ingredients until mixture is well blended. Serve at room temperature.

Makes about ¾ cup.

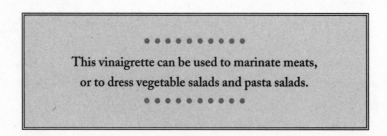

. . . .

This vinaigrette can be used to marinate meats,
or to dress vegetable salads and pasta salads.

. . . .

Low-Fat Creamy Herb Dressing

. . . .

VINAIGRETTES ARE GREAT ON SALADS, but sometimes I prefer a creamy dressing, like Thousand Island or blue cheese. You know: mayonnaise-laden, sour-cream laden.

This low-fat creamy herb dressing mimics the richness of fattier dressings and is loaded with the flavor of spicy horseradish and dill. It's delicious plain or with bits of feta cheese or blue cheese thrown in. Serve it on sturdy greens like romaine, not the flimsy, tender mixed greens you pay dearly for. Or use this dressing as a topping for baked potatoes, a dip for fresh vegetables or as a sauce for cooked vegetables.

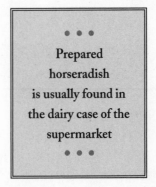

1   cup low-fat or nonfat cottage cheese
2   green onions, trimmed and coarsely chopped
1   large garlic clove
2   tablespoons vinegar (any kind)
2   teaspoons prepared horseradish
1   teaspoon dried dill
½   teaspoon salt, or to taste
    About 2 tablespoons water, buttermilk
    or milk

. . .
Prepared
horseradish
is usually found in
the dairy case of the
supermarket
. . .

Combine cottage cheese, green onions, garlic, vinegar, horseradish, dill and salt in a blender and blend until smooth. Gradually add up to 2 tablespoons water, buttermilk or milk until dressing is the desired consistency.

The dressing will thicken a little more on standing; feel free to mix in a little more water, buttermilk or milk as needed. Taste and add more salt, if desired.

Makes about 1 cup.

Spinach Salad

· · · · · · · · · · · ·

THOSE WHO GREW UP EATING CANNED OR FROZEN SPINACH are delighted to learn that fresh spinach is delicious. This orange-raisin dressing avoids fat and complements the mild flavor of the spinach.

About 8 cups fresh spinach, washed and
    dried, tough stems removed
½   cup nonfat plain yogurt
1   tablespoon orange juice concentrate
¼   teaspoon salt
¼   cup raisins
2-3   tablespoons chopped walnuts
About 2 tablespoons chopped red onion

> · · ·
> A 10-ounce bag
> of spinach leaves and
> a 1-pound bunch
> both yield about 4
> cups, once you discard
> the stems and any
> slimy leaves.
> · · ·

Divide spinach among serving plates or place in a large bowl. Combine yogurt, orange juice and salt in a small bowl. Pour over spinach leaves. Scatter raisins, walnuts and chopped onion over top.

Serves 4.

Grape and Walnut Salad

• •

FRUIT CHUNKS ARE A NICE SURPRISE in an otherwise predictable tossed salad. Add the crunch of nuts, and your mouth will be thoroughly entertained.

Don't feel restricted by the nuts or fruits given here; use what's handy and what you like. Toasted almonds, pecans or hazelnuts will substitute well. A friend of mine makes this salad with orange sections and roasted peanuts.

I store nuts in the freezer so they don't go rancid. Frozen nuts take a little longer to toast than those at room temperature.

⅓ cup walnut pieces
1 head curly leaf lettuce, washed and dried
3 tablespoons vegetable oil or olive oil
1 tablespoon apple cider vinegar
1 teaspoon Dijon-style mustard
½ teaspoon salt
½ teaspoon sugar
1 cup halved seedless grapes, red or green

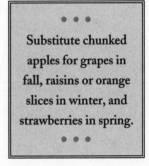

• • •
Substitute chunked apples for grapes in fall, raisins or orange slices in winter, and strawberries in spring.
• • •

Toast walnut pieces in a dry baking pan in a 400-degree oven until fragrant. They'll take 5 minutes in a preheated oven, longer if you put them in as the oven preheats. Remove and set aside to cool.

Tear lettuce into bite-size pieces and place in a large bowl.

In a small jar or bowl, shake or whisk oil, vinegar, mustard, salt and sugar. Drizzle over salad greens and toss. Top salad with grapes and toasted walnuts.

Serves 4 to 6.

Fresh Apple Salad

· ·

THIS APPLE SALAD IS A QUICK, low-fat version of the familiar Waldorf salad, without the walnuts and mayonnaise. The pineapple is optional, but it seems to please young diners.

2 large, firm unpeeled apples, cored
    and cut into chunks
1 8-ounce can unsweetened crushed pineapple
    with juice, drained (optional)
1 celery rib, trimmed and minced
½ cup plain yogurt
1-3 teaspoons sugar or honey, to taste

Place apple chunks in a medium-size bowl. Add pineapple (if using), celery and yogurt. Stir to blend. Sweeten with sugar or honey to taste.

Serves 4.

Cucumber-Yogurt Salad

· ·

CUCUMBER AND YOGURT IS A CLASSIC COMBINATION in Indian cuisine. This salad provides a cool counterpoint to hot curries.

1   8-ounce container plain yogurt (1 scant cup)
2   teaspoons dried mint or 2 tablespoons fresh
1   teaspoon dried dill or 1 tablespoon fresh
2   cucumbers, peeled, seeded and diced

Stir yogurt and herbs together in a medium-size bowl. Mix in cucumbers and serve, or refrigerate to chill.

Serves 4 to 6. ∾ Serve with burgers or other grilled meats and fish.

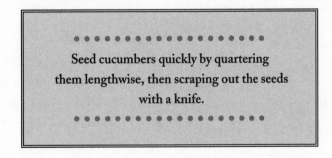

Seed cucumbers quickly by quartering
them lengthwise, then scraping out the seeds
with a knife.

Cherry Tomato-Mushroom Salad

· · · · · · · · · · · · · · · · ·

Gardeners know that cherry tomato plants are hardy and prolific. Although they have us screaming "uncle" before any other plant in the garden, with the possible exception of zucchini, they have their advantages. When larger store-bought tomatoes are inedible, cherry tomatoes can add a fresh taste to salad. The following salad keeps well refrigerated for 4 days.

¼ cup olive oil or vegetable oil
2 tablespoons red wine vinegar
1 teaspoon dried oregano
   Salt and freshly ground pepper
1 pint cherry tomatoes, halved
½ pound fresh mushrooms, sliced
   Leaf lettuce (optional)

· · ·

Leftovers can be added to green salad, used with cheese to fill pita bread, or added to a pasta salad.

· · ·

In a small jar with a tight-fitting lid, combine oil, vinegar, oregano, salt and pepper. Shake to combine.

Place cherry tomatoes in a bowl and add mushrooms. Toss with dressing and season to taste. Serve on a bed of lettuce, if desired.

Serves 6. ∾ Serve with grilled meats or as part of a salad sampler that includes a bean salad and pasta salad.

Carrot-Raisin Salad with Ginger

• • • • • • • • • • • • •

Carrot-raisin salad is a cinch if you have a food processor fitted with a grater. It's not much more difficult to make if you use a hand grater. Preparation tools need little more than a quick rinse to clean up, since there's nothing fatty or clingy to remove.

The typical cafeteria carrot-raisin salad is made with Miracle Whip or mayonnaise. I prefer the lively flavor of this one, which is moistened with a touch of yogurt. Ginger and honey complement the carrots. This salad is high in fiber and beta-carotene.

1 cup raisins
½ cup plain yogurt
1-2 tablespoons honey
Grated zest (yellow part of rind only)
of ½ lemon
1 teaspoon freshly squeezed lemon juice
1-2 teaspoons peeled, grated fresh ginger
4 cups peeled, grated carrots

• • •
Grate lemon
zest first, then
halve and
squeeze juice.
• • •

In a small bowl, cover raisins with hot water and set aside. In a medium-size bowl, mix yogurt, honey, lemon zest, lemon juice and ginger. Add carrots. Drain raisins and add, stirring to combine. This recipe doubles and triples easily. The salad will keep for several days in the refrigerator.

Serves 4 to 5.

Asparagus Salad

· · · · · · · · · · · · · · · · · · · ·

THERE'S NOTHING BETTER THAN FRESH ASPARAGUS. Cooked until bright green and firm but tender and drizzled with a well-made dressing, it can be the focus of a spring meal. Don't worry about how thick or thin the stalks are—any size is delicious as long as the tips are closed and the stalks look plump, not shriveled.

2 pounds asparagus, trimmed,
  tough stems peeled
1 large egg (optional)
3 tablespoons red wine vinegar
2½ tablespoons sugar
1½ teaspoons Dijon-style mustard
½ teaspoon paprika
¼ teaspoon salt
⅔ cup vegetable oil

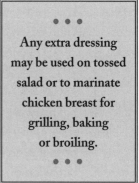

· · ·

Any extra dressing may be used on tossed salad or to marinate chicken breast for grilling, baking or broiling.

· · ·

In a large pot of boiling water, cook asparagus for 5 minutes. (Thin asparagus will cook more quickly.) It should be bright green and slightly crunchy, not limp. Drain and rinse with cold water; set aside. (Asparagus may be prepared ahead up to this point and refrigerated for 1 to 2 days.)

In the bowl of a food processor fitted with a steel blade or a blender or with a portable mixer, combine egg (if using), vinegar, sugar, mustard, paprika and salt. Blend until sugar is dissolved, about 2 minutes. Drizzle in oil in a slow, steady stream. If egg is used, the mixture will be viscous, but not thick like mayonnaise. If no egg is used, it will be thinner and may need a little more oil to reduce its tartness. Taste and correct for seasoning. Drizzle some dressing over asparagus and serve either lukewarm, at room temperature or chilled.

Serves 6 to 8.

Broccoli Salad

· · · · · · · · · · · · ·

Aᴌᴛʜᴏᴜɢʜ ᴍᴀɴʏ ᴄᴏᴏᴋs ᴀʀᴇ sᴜsᴘɪᴄɪᴏᴜs ᴏғ ᴀɴᴄʜᴏᴠɪᴇs, I like to think of them as Italian bouillon cubes. While you would never dream of eating a chicken bouillon cube by itself, you wouldn't hesitate to use it as a flavoring agent. So it is with anchovies, which add a salty earthiness to many dishes without overpowering them with a fishy taste. Caesar salad loses much of its appeal without the anchovies. So would this broccoli salad. If you're still suspicious of anchovies, prepare the broccoli as described and use your favorite dressing.

1½   pounds broccoli (1 medium head),
       trimmed and broken into florets
½   cup chopped fresh parsley
1-2 anchovy fillets
      Juice of 1 lemon
      Freshly ground pepper
¼   cup olive oil

· · ·
This recipe keeps well in the refrigerator. Add leftovers to cooked spiral pasta to make pasta salad.
· · ·

Cut broccoli florets into bite-size pieces. (You should have about 4 cups.) Briefly cook in boiling water over high heat until they are bright green but still very crunchy, about 5 minutes. Rinse with cold water, drain well and refrigerate immediately.

In a blender or food processor, puree parsley, anchovies, lemon juice and pepper. (If you don't have a blender, smush anchovies with a fork, then mix in remaining ingredients.) Slowly add oil until mixture thickens.

Pour dressing over broccoli and toss gently.

Serves 4.

Cauliflower Salad

CAULIFLOWER AND BROCCOLI ARE CRUCIFEROUS VEGETABLES. Health specialists believe they protect us against cancer (other crucifers include Brussels sprouts, cabbage, bok choy, kohlrabi and turnips).

This salad holds well in the refrigerator, so it can be made ahead of time and chilled until you need it.

1 medium head cauliflower, broken into florets
1 red bell pepper, cored, seeded and diced
¼ cup sliced black olives, preferably imported, packed in brine
3 tablespoons olive oil
1 tablespoon red wine vinegar
1 teaspoon dried oregano
1 teaspoon salt, or to taste
¼ teaspoon freshly ground pepper

> • • •
> Imported black olives that are packed in glass jars taste far better than the California-style pitted canned variety. They are more trouble, but worth it.
> • • •

In a large pot of boiling water, cook cauliflower over high heat for 5 minutes, or until tender. Drain and immediately rinse with cold water to cool. Drain completely and place in a large bowl.

Add red pepper and olives to cauliflower.

In a small jar or bowl, combine oil, vinegar, oregano, salt and pepper. Shake or whisk to blend well and pour over cauliflower.

Chill, if desired. This salad keeps for several days refrigerated.

Serves 8 generously.

Cabbage Salad

· · · · · · · · · · · · ·

Jacques Pépin, cooking teacher, author and former chef to French presidents, rose to a challenge I once set for him: to create dinner for 6, for $10 or less, in 1 hour, after shopping for less than 30 minutes. Swiftly, he assembled a spicy roasted beef, sweet potatoes, sautéed zucchini, cabbage salad, poached apples and rolls.

   Within 61 minutes, he was getting his picture taken with the huge menu. This was the cabbage salad he made—a European coleslaw with a vinaigrette. Pépin says this salad may sit a while so it can soften. It keeps for several days in the refrigerator.

1	medium head Savoy cabbage
¼	cup olive oil
1½	tablespoons wine vinegar or cider vinegar
1½	tablespoons Dijon-style mustard
½	teaspoon Worcestershire sauce
2	garlic cloves, minced, or to taste
	Salt and freshly ground pepper

Slice cabbage into shreds (discard core); you should have about 9 cups.
In a large bowl, combine remaining ingredients and blend well (sauce will separate; that's fine).
Add cabbage and toss. Season to taste with salt and pepper.

Serves 6 to 8.

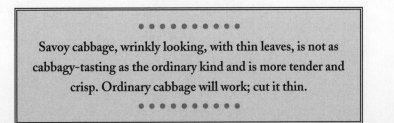

· · · · · · · · · · ·

Savoy cabbage, wrinkly looking, with thin leaves, is not as cabbagy-tasting as the ordinary kind and is more tender and crisp. Ordinary cabbage will work; cut it thin.

· · · · · · · · · · ·

Black-Eyed Pea Salad

• •

THE COMBINATION OF BLACK-EYED PEAS AND DILL PICKLES struck me as just a tad bizarre when I first encountered it. To be polite, I tasted it and loved it. Serve this salad as part of a salad-sampler plate with pasta salad and a vegetable salad. Or serve it with hot corn bread or a biscuit or roll and a lettuce salad as a cool summer lunch or dinner. This recipe is from Marty Godbey, author of dining guidebooks.

1   15-ounce can black-eyed peas with
    jalapeño peppers
½   cup diced celery
¼   cup diced dill pickle
2   tablespoons diced red bell pepper
2   tablespoons mayonnaise

Drain black-eyed peas and rinse under cold running water. Remove any bits of jalapeño or fat; place black-eyed peas in a bowl.

Add remaining ingredients and stir to blend, adding pickle juice to thin and season, if necessary. Chill before serving, if you have time, or serve right away.

Serves 4.

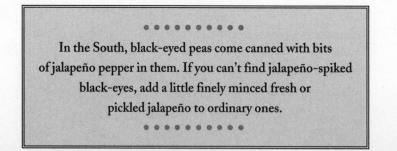

• • • • • • • • • •

In the South, black-eyed peas come canned with bits
of jalapeño pepper in them. If you can't find jalapeño-spiked
black-eyes, add a little finely minced fresh or
pickled jalapeño to ordinary ones.

• • • • • • • • • •

Summer Salad

• • • • • • • • • • • • •

ONE OF THE WORLD'S GREAT FOOD TRAVESTIES is the winter tomato. Please don't make this salad in the winter, when it will have little flavor.

Make it often in the summer, however, when the clean juiciness of vine-ripened tomatoes is a perfect partner for rich, smooth avocados. It's the same theory the Italians use when they pair tomatoes and fresh mozzarella cheese.

For an attractive arrangement, fan the avocado slices over the top of the plate and place the tomato slices on top. Or dice the tomatoes and avocado and toss them gently together.

3-4	tablespoons olive oil
	Juice of 1 lime
	Salt and freshly ground pepper to taste
2-3	avocados, peeled and pitted
3	medium tomatoes, sliced
2	tablespoons minced fresh cilantro (also called coriander or Chinese parsley)
2	tablespoons minced green onions

Combine olive oil and lime juice with salt and pepper in a small bowl.
Slice avocados and coat with lime-juice mixture. Arrange on plates with sliced tomatoes.
Sprinkle with cilantro and green onions.

Serves 6.

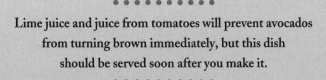

> • • • • • • • • •
>
> Lime juice and juice from tomatoes will prevent avocados
> from turning brown immediately, but this dish
> should be served soon after you make it.
>
> • • • • • • • • •

Tomato Salad with Feta Cheese

· ·

VINE RIPE means something different to commercial tomato growers than it does to you and me. It doesn't mean the tomato turned red on the vine. It means a tomato that is picked green but will turn red by the time it reaches you, or maybe sometime after that. Use fresh, locally grown tomatoes that really *are* ripened on the vine for this recipe. When they are not available, substitute cherry tomatoes.

This salad goes well with chicken that has been seasoned with dried oregano, salt and pepper before it is baked. It also complements flank steak, hamburgers and grilled or broiled fish. If you have leftovers, toss them into a pita sandwich. Or add leftover fish, chicken or flank steak to the salad and serve as a main-dish salad or a sandwich filling.

3   medium tomatoes, cored
1   medium cucumber, peeled and diced; seeded,
       if desired
6-7   imported black olives, pitted (substitute
       green olives rather than use canned black
       olives), coarsely chopped
4   ounces feta cheese (about ¾ cup crumbled)
3   tablespoons olive oil
1   tablespoon red wine vinegar or
       apple cider vinegar
     Salt and freshly ground pepper
     Leaf lettuce (optional)

Chop tomatoes into 1-inch pieces. Add cucumbers and olives.

Crumble feta cheese over vegetable; drizzle with olive oil and vinegar. Add salt and pepper to taste just before serving. (This salad may not need much salt because feta is very salty.) Serve on a bed of lettuce, if desired.

Serves 6 generously.

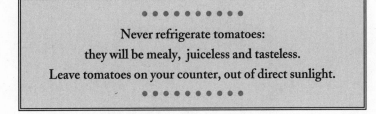

Never refrigerate tomatoes:
they will be mealy, juiceless and tasteless.
Leave tomatoes on your counter, out of direct sunlight.

Beef, Lamb & Pork

· · · · · · · · · · · · ·

EXPLAIN THIS TO ME: why do people in a rush to put dinner on the table stop at fast-food restaurants for burgers and fries? Of all the foods I would pay someone else to cook, ground beef is at the bottom of the list. It's a family-pleasing, instant dinner and takes no effort. I'll make the burgers myself and bake fries while they cook, saving my money for foods I can't easily reproduce at home.

Burgers are no longer served as often as they once were, since concerns about fat have crowded meat off the center of the plate. That's good, but small amounts are great for adding flavor and substance to a meal. If we learn to use meat judiciously, serving leaner cuts, adding it as a seasoning in a dish or to bolster a pile of rice or a stack of tortillas, meat can be healthful and a boon to the busy cook.

I like to season pasta and rice dishes with about ¼ cup minced country ham. Thinly sliced flank steak makes a great sub, with tomatoes and onions on thick bread. Chunks of tender lamb or pork cook quickly and make a tasty, filling topping for couscous or rice. Pork tenderloin, which has less fat than chicken breast, cooks in just 30 minutes.

CUTTING MEAT INTO SMALLER pieces and turning up the heat can hasten cooking. Ground chuck (hamburger) cooks in minutes; whole chuck takes hours. My mother's roasted leg of lamb tastes great but takes forever to cook. Instead, I ask the butcher to bone the lamb leg, and then I broil or grill it; it's ready in a fraction of the time. Similarly, beef chuck cut into 2-inch cubes takes hours to cook in stew; in 1-inch cubes, it takes less than an hour. Single-portion meat loaves cook more quickly than large loaves.

Keep portions appropriately small by slicing meat thinly. Cut pork tenderloin and flank steak on the diagonal, so the slices look bigger. Not only will the dinner be more healthful, but you may have leftovers to give you a head start on tomorrow night's dinner.

Cheeseburger Casserole

· ·

YOU'VE GOT TO HAND IT TO CASSEROLES: they sure come in handy. They can be assembled ahead of time, reheated when you need them and prove willing receptacles for leftovers; they are the meal-in-a-dish prototype.

· · ·

To speed up this recipe, serve it right from the saucepan with a sprinkling of cheese on top.

· · ·

1   pound ground beef
1   medium onion, minced
1   green bell pepper, cored and minced
1   28-ounce can chopped tomatoes, with juice
1   tablespoon Worcestershire sauce
1   teaspoon dried oregano
    Salt to taste
4   cups (8 ounces) medium egg noodles
1½ cups grated Cheddar cheese

In a large skillet, cook beef over medium heat, stirring occasionally to break up clumps, until brown all over. Drain excess fat.

Increase heat to high, add onion and green pepper and cook for 5 minutes, stirring. Add tomatoes and their juice, Worcestershire sauce, oregano and salt. Bring to a boil, lower heat to low and simmer, uncovered, while you bring a large pot of water to a boil.

Preheat the oven to 350 degrees. Boil noodles until quite tender, about 6 minutes; drain.

Return noodles to the pot and stir in ground-beef mixture. (It should be fairly dry, not soupy.) Pour into a casserole dish and top with cheese. Bake until cheese melts, about 10 minutes if beef mixture is hot, 20 minutes or more if it has been refrigerated.

Serves 6 generously. ∾ **Serve with steamed asparagus or broccoli.**

Cajun Burgers

· · · · · · · · · · · · · ·

W<small>E HAVE</small> C<small>AJUN CHEFS TO THANK</small> for teaching us how to combine a bunch of shelf-handy spices into the highly seasoned mixtures they use for "blackening." The following recipe is for asbestos palates; if yours is more delicate, begin with half the seasoning recommended below.

1	pound lean ground beef
1	tablespoon garlic powder
1	tablespoon paprika
1	tablespoon onion powder
1	teaspoon freshly ground pepper
2	teaspoons salt
	Pinch cayenne pepper (optional)
1-2	tablespoons vegetable oil for cooking patties

Form ground beef into 4 patties.

Combine spices, salt and pepper in a small bowl. Sprinkle both sides of patties with spice mixture, covering them. Cover and chill until ready to use, or cook immediately.

To fry, heat a large skillet on high heat and add a little oil to lightly cover the bottom of the pan. Add patties and brown on both sides until cooked through, or grill under the broiler or outdoors.

Serves 4. ∽ **Serve with oven-baked French fries (page 165).**

Variation

Flank Steak Creole: Substitute flank steak for ground beef and rub in the spices. Grill or broil the steak to rare, about 4 to 6 minutes total. Slice thinly against the grain.

Italian "Sausage" Burgers

· ·

EVERYONE ASSOCIATES SAUSAGE WITH FAT and with good reason: it usually is loaded with it. Consequently, many people avoid sausage. Too bad, because it tastes great and cooks quickly. Here, lean beef is combined with traditional sausage seasonings like red pepper and fennel. These burgers are easy, full-flavored, cook quickly and can be addictive.

1	pound lean ground beef
1½	teaspoons paprika
½	teaspoon crushed red pepper flakes
½	teaspoon fennel seeds
½	teaspoon salt
¼	teaspoon dried thyme
¼	teaspoon freshly ground pepper
1	garlic clove, minced
1	8-ounce can tomato sauce (1 scant cup, optional; you'll have leftovers)
4	thin slices mozzarella cheese

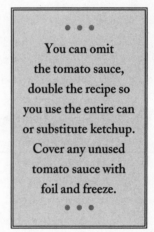

· · ·

You can omit the tomato sauce, double the recipe so you use the entire can or substitute ketchup. Cover any unused tomato sauce with foil and freeze.

· · ·

Preheat the broiler, with a rack 5 inches from the heat source.

Place beef in a large bowl and mix in seasonings and garlic.

Form into 4 patties, about ½ inch thick. Place patties in a shallow baking dish and place under the broiler. Cook for 5 minutes, turn, top with a spoonful of tomato sauce, if using, and a slice of cheese. Cook for 5 minutes more, or until cheese bubbles.

Serve immediately.

Serves 4. ∽ Serve with spiral noodles and steamed green beans.

Small Meat Loaves

• •

SOMETIMES A CHANGE IN TECHNIQUE can decrease cooking time and get old-fashioned dishes back on the table. Meat loaves are traditionally made with 1½ to 2 pounds of ground meat and take at least an hour to bake. But if you form a little less meat into smaller loaves, you can get the same flavor in about one-third the time. I also speed things up by mixing everything in a single bowl.

These meat loaves are delicious hot, and the leftovers make good sandwiches.

2	slices white or whole wheat bread
⅓	cup milk or beef broth
1	large egg
2	tablespoons minced parsley, preferably fresh
1	teaspoon salt
1	garlic clove, minced, or 1 tablespoon grated onion (optional)
½	teaspoon freshly ground pepper
1	pound lean ground beef

Preheat the oven to 375 degrees.

Crumble bread into a large bowl and add milk or beef broth. When bread is soft, about 1 to 2 minutes, mash it with a fork or your hands. Add egg, parsley, salt, garlic or onion (if using) and pepper; beat together to blend.

Add ground beef and mix only enough to blend evenly. Form into 4 small loaves, about 5 by 2½ inches; place on a lightly oiled, shallow cookie sheet.

Bake for 20 minutes, or until loaves are cooked through.

Serves 4. ❧ **Serve with boiled potatoes or rice and braised greens or red cabbage.**

Variations

Italian Meat Loaf: Add 1 teaspoon dried basil and 1 teaspoon dried oregano to the meat mixture, along with ¼ cup Parmesan cheese. Form into loaves as directed. If desired, top with Italian tomato sauce. Bake as directed. Serve with boiled noodles and sliced onions and green peppers sautéed in olive oil.

Steak House Meat Loaf: Add 1 tablespoon grated horseradish and 2 tablespoons ketchup or chili sauce to the meat mixture. Form into loaves. If desired, place ½ slice bacon on top of each loaf and bake as directed.

Mexican Baked Potatoes

· ·

Baked potatoes are effortless—just wash and bake. You can top them with butter or sour cream, but there are heartier, more healthful toppings that make more of a meal. The following one from Tex-Mex cuisine relies on convenient canned "chili beans," also called "chili hot beans." They are canned in a spicy but not hot chili sauce that adds extra oomph to them.

4   large baking potatoes
1   pound lean ground beef
1   medium onion, chopped
1   16-ounce can chili beans
1   4-ounce can chopped mild green chilies
¾   cup bottled chunky salsa
½   teaspoon ground cumin
     Grated Cheddar or Monterey Jack cheese
1   avocado, peeled, pitted and chopped
     (optional)

> · · ·
> This amount of topping is perfect for the large potatoes that are sold singly. If you use smaller ones, bake more, or plan on leftover topping.
> · · ·

Preheat the oven to 450 degrees. Place potatoes on a cookie sheet and bake for 30 minutes. Puncture with a fork and bake until tender, about 30 minutes more.

Brown beef in a large skillet on medium-high heat, stirring occasionally to break up clumps; drain fat.

Add onions and cook until soft, about 10 to 15 minutes. Add chili beans, green chilies, salsa and cumin; heat through.

Split baked potatoes in half and pour meat mixture over them. Top with grated cheese and chopped avocado, if you have a ripe one.

Serves 4, with lots of topping.   ❧   **Serve with a simple salad made of green leaf lettuce and an oil-and-vinegar dressing seasoned with Dijon-style mustard.**

Garlic Flank Steak

· ·

HERE'S A GREAT MARINADE for flank steak. Any unused vinaigrette will keep for months refrigerated and can be used to marinate virtually any meat before grilling, baking or broiling—try it on lamb chops, pork chops, fish or chicken. Or it can also be used to dress tossed salad or lightly cooked vegetables such as broccoli, green beans or cauliflower.

4	large garlic cloves, peeled and flattened
1	cup olive oil
⅓	cup red wine vinegar
1	tablespoon Dijon-style mustard
1	teaspoon salt
½	teaspoon freshly ground pepper
1	1½-to-2-pound flank steak or sirloin steak

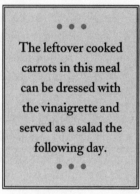

· · ·

The leftover cooked carrots in this meal can be dressed with the vinaigrette and served as a salad the following day.

· · ·

Preheat the broiler, with a rack about 3 inches from the heat source.

Place garlic in a jar with a tight-fitting lid or in a small bowl. Add oil, vinegar and seasonings. Shake or whisk to combine.

Score the steak at right angles to the grain, about ⅛ inch deep on both sides. Combine ½ cup dressing with steak in a plastic bag and secure with a twist tie (or place steak on a large plate and drizzle with the dressing). Allow to marinate for up to 20 minutes at room temperature or up to 2 days in the refrigerator. (Return to room temperature before continuing.)

Broil for 3 to 4 minutes on each side. (Steak should be cooked no more than medium-rare—it is a lean cut that will become tough when overcooked.) Cut across the grain into ¼-inch-thick slices.

Serves 4, with leftovers. ⌒ **Serve with rice with pecans (page 174) and cooked carrots.**

Tex-Mex Barley Hotdish

• •

Quick-cooking barley is a whole grain that cooks as quickly as rice, so it is useful to the harried cook. Its chewy nuttiness provides a nice change for even the most finicky diners.

1	pound lean ground beef
2	medium onions, chopped
3	garlic cloves, minced
1	16-ounce can garbanzo beans (chickpeas), undrained
1	28-ounce can tomatoes, chopped
1	teaspoon chili powder
1	teaspoon ground cumin
½	teaspoon dried oregano
1½	cups uncooked quick-cooking barley
1	cup water
	Salt and freshly ground pepper to taste
1	cup grated Cheddar cheese

In a large saucepan or Dutch oven, brown ground beef, stirring occasionally to break up clumps, for about 5 to 10 minutes. Drain all fat and add onions and garlic. Cook for about 5 minutes, stirring occasionally, until softened.

Add garbanzo beans, tomatoes with juice, chili powder, cumin and oregano. Stir in barley, water, salt and pepper. Stir briefly; cover and simmer for 20 to 30 minutes, or until barley is tender.

Serve topped with cheese.

Serves 6 generously.   ∾   **Serve with tossed salad or cooked spinach.**

Variation

To bake: After simmering barley, spoon mixture into a casserole dish, sprinkle with cheese and bake at 400 degrees for 15 minutes, or until cheese is melted. (The casserole may be frozen before baking. Cool, sprinkle with cheese and wrap, label and freeze for up to 3 months. Heat oven to 350 degrees, cover casserole with foil and bake for 1 hour, or until heated through and cheese is bubbly.)

California Flank Steak

● ●

FLANK STEAK IS A SOLID ENTRY in the repertoire of rushed cooks. It tastes fabulous, has great "chew" and is ready in less than 10 minutes.

The herbed cheese topping here adds flavor to beef and is a real surprise for people who only are used to eating steak marinated and broiled, period.

You need a creamy-ish cheese that stands up to the flavor of beef. My family loves blue, but feta is lower in fat, less expensive and delicious. Our Italian deli sells a great creamy feta, but sometimes we're stuck with the crumbly supermarket kind. In that case, I use a fork to mix the feta with a little sour cream, cream or cream cheese—just enough to spread it on the steak. If your cheese is creamy enough to spread, forgo the cream.

Though flank steak looks like a lot of food to someone cooking for 2 or 3 people, don't underestimate the leftovers. The steak makes delicious sandwiches when served on French or poppy seed rolls with sliced onion, tomato and mustard.

1	1½-to-2-pound flank steak
1	tablespoon olive oil
½	teaspoon dried thyme or oregano
½	teaspoon salt
¼	pound feta cheese (or your favorite creamy fresh goat cheese or blue cheese)
2	tablespoons minced fresh parsley (optional)
1	garlic clove, minced
¼	teaspoon freshly ground pepper
1	tablespoon sour cream or cream (optional)

Rub each side of steak with oil, thyme or oregano and salt; set aside. Preheat the broiler, with a rack about 3 inches from the heat source.

Crumble cheese in a small bowl and add parsley (if using), garlic and pepper. Mash with a fork (you may need to add a little sour cream or cream to moisten the mixture); set aside.

Place flank steak on a broiler pan and broil for 2 minutes. Turn and broil for another 2 minutes; the meat should still be rare inside.

Spread with cheese mixture, if using, and broil for 2 minutes more, or until bubbly.

Slice steak thinly at right angles to the grain of the meat.

Serves 6. ◡ **Serve with noodles and cooked carrots.**

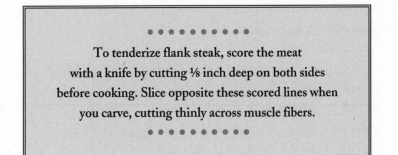

• • • • • • • • • •

To tenderize flank steak, score the meat
with a knife by cutting ⅛ inch deep on both sides
before cooking. Slice opposite these scored lines when
you carve, cutting thinly across muscle fibers.

• • • • • • • • • •

Derby Day Tenderloin

. . . .

BEEF TENDERLOIN IS THE FIRST CHOICE of hosts and hostesses serving a fancy dinner because it's the tenderest cut and the easiest to deal with: you just put it in a pan and roast it. It cooks quickly too. As a result, it is a fixture of brunch and dinner tables all over Louisville during Kentucky Derby festivities.

    1   tenderloin of beef (about 4 pounds)
    2   tablespoons olive oil
    ½   teaspoon dried thyme
    ½   teaspoon dried oregano
    ½   teaspoon dried basil

Preheat the oven to 500 degrees. Fold narrow end of beef under so that the roast is of uniform thickness; rub with oil. If using a regular meat thermometer, insert the thermometer diagonally into center of tenderloin.

Place tenderloin on a rack in a roasting pan and place in the oven. Immediately reduce heat to 400 degrees and bake for 15 minutes.

Meanwhile, combine olive oil with herbs. Rub or brush mixture on meat and bake for 15 minutes more—it should roast a total of 30 minutes and the thermometer should register 130 degrees for rare.

Let stand a few minutes before carving so the juices can settle.

Serves 10.   ~ **Serve with Savory Broccoli (page 159) and baked potatoes.**

Herbed Blade Roast

● ●

BLADE ROAST IS ONE OF THOSE CUTS that demands long, slow simmering. It's the perfect choice for a pot roast. But in my family, we don't have time for that, but we love blade roast because it's inexpensive and "meaty." So I treat it like flank steak. Sear it quickly on the outside, slice it thinly against the grain and you'll tenderize and add flavor at the same time.

1½	teaspoons salt
1	teaspoon dried thyme
1	teaspoon dried oregano
½	teaspoon ground cayenne pepper
¼	teaspoon ground coriander
⅛	teaspoon ground allspice
1	3-pound shoulder blade roast
1	tablespoon olive oil
2-3	tablespoons water

Preheat the oven to 450 degrees. Combine seasonings in a small bowl. Coat meat on both sides with seasonings, rubbing them in.

Heat a large cast-iron skillet over high heat. Add oil and heat for 30 seconds. Add meat and sear quickly on all sides, about 2 minutes each. Set the skillet in the oven and roast meat, uncovered, for about 15 or 20 minutes for medium-rare.

Remove from the oven, transfer meat to a cutting board and let stand for 10 minutes before slicing.

Meanwhile, to make gravy, pour water into the hot skillet and cook over medium-high heat, stirring to loosen all the bits remaining in the bottom.

Slice meat thinly on a slant with a very sharp knife. Pour gravy over meat.

Serves 6 to 8 generously. ∽ **Serve with broiled buttered zucchini and egg noodles.**

Lamb with Mustard Marinade

· ·

LAMB IS NATURALLY TENDER because it comes from a young animal, and it is enormously flavorful. Cuts from the tenderest parts—the leg and the loin—cook quickly and without demanding much effort from the cook. The full flavor of this trusty marinade seasons the meat immediately; there's no need to let it sit before broiling.

Accompany the lamb with tomato-mushroom skewers: Toss 1 pint cherry tomatoes and ½ pound mushrooms (cut to the size of cherry tomatoes, if large) with the lamb marinade, place in a broiling pan and broil alongside the meat.

2	tablespoons Dijon-style mustard
1	tablespoon soy sauce
	Juice of 1 lemon
1	teaspoon dried thyme
½	teaspoon salt
1	small garlic clove, minced
1	pound cubed lamb, cut from the leg

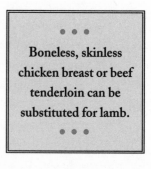

· · ·

Boneless, skinless chicken breast or beef tenderloin can be substituted for lamb.

· · ·

Preheat the broiler, with a rack 5 inches from the heat source. Lightly grease the broiler pan.

Combine mustard, soy, lemon, thyme, salt and garlic in a medium bowl. Add lamb and toss to coat; set aside. If using wooden skewers, soak them in water for at least 5 minutes so they don't burn under the broiler.

Thread lamb on skewers; place on the broiler pan.

Broil meat, turning once, cooking for about 5 minutes for medium-rare. (Broiling time will vary according to the temperature of the meat, the size of the chunks and how tightly they are packed on the skewers.)

Serve each skewer on a plate.

Serves 4. ∾ Serve with rice and tomato-mushroom skewers.

Lamb Chops

· · · · · · · · · · ·

Lamb chops are the perfect splurge food—rich enough to be satisfying, expensive enough to be decadent, small enough to be within healthy guidelines. Save them for special times.

Please note: The cooking time for the chops will vary depending on how cold the chops are, how thick they are, how much bone they have and how hot the heat is.

>   4   loin lamb chops
>   Salt and freshly ground pepper

Preheat the grill or broiler, with a rack 3 inches from the heat source.

Grill chops or broil them on a rack set in a pan, turning once, for about 3 minutes on each side for rare. Transfer to a warm platter and season with salt and pepper.

Serves 2 . ∾ **Serve with buttered green beans and rice with mushrooms.**

Lamb and Rice Casserole

· ·

THE COMBINATION OF MIDDLE EASTERN SPICES makes this dish unusual but not difficult to prepare. I like it best in autumn or winter, served with sweet potatoes or winter squash.

To cook squash: Halve squash lengthwise from stem to tip; scoop out and discard seeds. Place face down on a greased cookie sheet and bake at 375 degrees for 45 minutes, or until tender.

2	tablespoons vegetable oil
1	onion, minced
2	teaspoons ground cumin
2	teaspoons ground cinnamon
½	teaspoon ground cayenne pepper
1	pound ground lamb or turkey
1	14-ounce can crushed tomatoes
1	14-to-16-ounce can (about 2 cups) beef broth
⅓	cup dried currants or raisins
1	cup raw long-grain white rice
	Salt to taste
	Crumbled feta or grated Parmesan cheese

Heat oil over medium heat in a large skillet or Dutch oven. Add onion, cumin, cinnamon and cayenne pepper and cook until onion is soft, about 15 minutes.

Meanwhile, cook lamb or turkey in a medium-size dish in the microwave or in a medium skillet over medium heat, stirring occasionally to break up clumps; drain all fat. Add lamb to the skillet with the seasonings, along with tomatoes, beef broth, currants or raisins, rice and salt. Bring to a boil over high heat, reduce heat to low, cover and simmer gently until rice is cooked, about 20 minutes.

Serve topped with crumbled feta cheese or Parmesan.

Serves 4. ∾ **Serve with baked winter squash or sweet potatoes, or with Brussels sprouts sautéed in olive oil and seasoned with lemon juice.**

· · · · · · · · · · ·
If you're serving the meal with baked winter squash or sweet potatoes, put them in the oven before you begin the casserole.
· · · · · · · · · · ·

Lamb Ragout

• • • • • • • • • • • •

OLD-FASHIONED DISHES LIKE STEW seem impossible when we're cramped for time, but there are techniques that make these dishes quick to prepare. In the case of stew, choose tender cuts and use smaller pieces. A 2½-inch chunk of lamb may take as long as 1½ hours to become tender, but a 1-inch chunk tenderizes in a much shorter time. Lamb leg meat is tender even before it is cooked; shoulder is cheaper and tougher, but cut small, it cooks quickly.

Lamb ragout is just a fancy name for stew. Expect the luscious gravy and flavor you get with any good stew.

2 tablespoons olive oil
2 medium onions, diced
1 garlic clove, minced
2 pounds lamb leg meat or shoulder,
     cut into cubes, or lamb stewing meat
2 tablespoons all-purpose flour
2 tablespoons tomato paste
1 14-to-16-ounce can (about 2 cups)
     chicken broth or 1½ cups water
     and ½ cup white wine
½ teaspoon dried thyme
     Salt and lots of freshly ground
       pepper to taste
3 carrots, peeled and cut into 2-inch lengths

• • •

Browning lamb
in batches develops
the best flavor in
the meat.

• • •

Heat oil in a Dutch oven over high heat. Add onions and garlic and sauté for 4 minutes on high heat, stirring occasionally, until softened.

On a large plate, toss lamb with flour. Add lamb to the Dutch oven, a few pieces at a time, and

sauté, turning to brown on all sides; transfer to a large plate. When all lamb is browned, return it to the Dutch oven and stir in tomato paste, chicken broth or water and wine, thyme, salt and pepper. Bring to a boil, cover, reduce heat to low and simmer for 20 minutes.

Add carrots and place the lid slightly ajar so that some of the steam can escape. Simmer for at least 20 or up to 40 minutes more, until lamb is tender.

Serves 6. ⌒ **Serve over cooked rice or noodles and with chopped cucumbers tossed with sour cream and a little minced onion, salt and pepper.**

Dry-Rubbed Pork Chops

· ·

DRY RUBS ADD FLAVOR to all kinds of food without adding extra fat. This flavorful mix combines sage and ginger.

> 1   teaspoon rubbed sage leaves
> 1   teaspoon ground ginger
> 1   teaspoon salt
> ½   teaspoon freshly ground pepper
> 4   pork chops, 1½ inches thick
> 1   tablespoon vegetable oil or olive oil

Combine sage, ginger, salt and pepper in a small bowl. Rub a little of the mixture on both sides of the pork chops.

Heat oil on high heat in a skillet wide enough to hold pork chops. Add pork chops, reduce heat to medium and brown on one side. Turn pork chops, cover and cook for 20 minutes, or until cooked through; meat should be pale, showing only the barest trace of pink.

Serves 4.   ∾   Serve with rice and tomato salad.

Baked Pork Chops

· ·

PORK LOIN CHOPS ARE TENDER AND JUICY, a perfect choice for quick baking. Remember how cookbooks used to recommend cooking pork chops for an hour? No wonder pork got a bad name. These chops cook quickly on high heat in just 20 minutes. Mustard and tarragon do wonders for pork.

1	tablespoon olive oil
4	pork loin chops, about ¾ inch thick
1	tablespoon red wine vinegar
1	tablespoon Dijon-style or Pommery mustard
1	teaspoon dried tarragon
½	teaspoon salt
	Pinch of freshly ground pepper

Preheat the oven to 450 degrees.

Oil a baking dish large enough to hold chops in a single layer; place chops in the dish. Combine remaining ingredients in a small bowl and place a spoonful on each pork chop.

Cover the dish with a lid or foil and bake for 10 minutes. Remove cover, turn chops and bake, uncovered, for 10 minutes more, or until meat is cooked through but juicy.

Serves 4. ◡ Serve with potatoes and cherry tomato salad or green beans.

Honey-Glazed Grilled Pork

. . . .

ASIAN COOKS KNOW HOW TO TANTALIZE a palate, with a sauce containing something sweet, something tart, some salty soy sauce and aromatics like ginger and garlic. Dry sherry continues the Chinese theme in this pork chop dinner. If you can't get it at the supermarket, the chops will be fine without it.

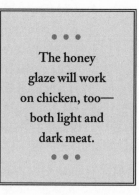

½ cup honey
2 tablespoons soy sauce
2 tablespoons dry white wine or dry sherry (optional)
2 tablespoons freshly squeezed lemon juice
2 tablespoons minced green onions
2 garlic cloves, minced
1 tablespoon peeled, minced fresh ginger
Salt and freshly ground pepper to taste
6 pork chops, about ¾-1 inch thick

> . . .
> The honey glaze will work on chicken, too— both light and dark meat.
> . . .

Combine all ingredients except meat in a large bowl. Add pork chops; toss to coat with marinade. Cover and refrigerate for at least 20 minutes or up to 24 hours.

Preheat the broiler or grill, with a rack 4 inches from the heat source.

Broil or grill for 15 minutes, turn, and cook for 10 minutes more, or until juices run clear when pork is pricked with a fork.

Serves 6. ∾ Serve with rice and Sesame Green Beans (page 157).

Variation

Honey-Glazed Chicken: Substitute 2½ to 3 pounds chicken pieces for pork. Cook, skin side up, for 15 minutes, turn, and cook for 10 to 15 minutes more, or until meat is cooked through and juices run clear when meat is pierced with a knife.

Pork Chops Niçoise

· ·

ANYTHING NIÇOISE SOUNDS DELICIOUS TO ME: salty olives and tomatoes are good on almost anything. Garlic wouldn't hurt this dish a bit either.

> 1   tablespoon vegetable oil
> 4   pork loin chops, 1 inch thick
> 1   28-ounce can tomatoes
> ½   teaspoon salt
> ½   teaspoon crushed red pepper flakes
> ¼   teaspoon freshly ground pepper
> 2   tablespoons sliced whole imported black or
>   stuffed green olives

> · · ·
>
> If you want to add minced garlic, do so after browning the chops but before adding the tomatoes.
>
> · · ·

Heat oil over medium-high heat in a skillet large enough to hold pork chops in a single layer (or use 2 skillets to brown chops and combine them later). Add pork chops and brown well on both sides, for 3 to 5 minutes per side. Drain any excess fat.

Crush tomatoes by squeezing them through your fingers into the skillet. Add salt, red pepper flakes and pepper. Bring to a boil, reduce heat to low and simmer, uncovered, for 10 minutes more.

Meanwhile, pit black olives or rinse and slice green olives. Add olives and simmer, uncovered, for another 10 to 15 minutes, until chops are done.

Serves 4. ∿ Serve with spaghetti or buttered noodles or spinach cooked in garlic butter.

Variation

You may substitute boneless, skinless chicken breasts for pork; they take less than 15 minutes to cook. You may want to remove them to serving plates after they cook and simmer the sauce, uncovered, to thicken it a little.

Quick Posole

· · · · · · · · · · · · · ·

Posole is a Southwestern dish—pronounced pah-SOL-ay—that combines hominy and tough cuts of fresh pork like the shoulder, and lots of chilies and spices. Ordinarily, of course, it takes a long time to cook. Substitute highly seasoned sausage for the pork shoulder and canned hominy for dried, and you make dinner in less than half an hour.

Canned hominy, available in many supermarkets in the South or Southwest, is made from dried corn that has been treated with lye to remove the hulls. It has a bland but haunting flavor, not unlike corn tortillas. It's truly wonderful.

1	pound hot Italian sausage or breakfast sausage
1	teaspoon ground cumin
1	green bell pepper, cored and chopped
1	onion, chopped
1	garlic clove, minced
1	jalapeño pepper, or to taste, seeded and minced
2	29-ounce cans white or yellow hominy, drained
1	4-ounce can chopped mild green chilies

> · · ·
>
> I make this recipe with bulk Italian sausage that yields 2 to 3 tablespoons of fat when fried. That's all you need for sautéing the vegetables.
>
> · · ·

Crumble sausage into a large skillet and cook, stirring, over medium heat. Stir in cumin. Add green pepper, onions, garlic and jalapeño pepper, stirring occasionally.

Add the hominy and cook to heat through. Stir in the green chilies.

Serves 4. ～ Serve in large bowls with warm flour tortillas or corn tortillas, tomato salsa and extra hot sauce, if desired.

Pork Fried Rice

· · · · · · · · · · · · · · · · · ·

PERFECT THE TECHNIQUE of "FRIED RICE," and you will never again be at the mercy of dinner hour. Never is a dangerous word, but if you can fry rice, you'll be able to make dinner with the barest of cupboards and fridges.

The technique is this: sauté or stir-fry well-seasoned meat and vegetables quickly and combine them with cooked white rice seasoned with soy sauce. This recipe uses pork and snow peas, but you can make it with leftover bits of baked chicken and a package of frozen mixed vegetables, or leave out the meat and cut up some carrots and toss in leftover broccoli. Eggs are traditional in fried rice. If you want to shave more time off this dish, scramble the eggs instead.

3   cups cooked white rice, preferably chilled,
       or 1½ cups raw long-grain white rice
1   tablespoon plus 1 teaspoon soy sauce,
       plus more for passing at the table
2   teaspoons sugar
2   teaspoons cornstarch
       Pinch of salt and freshly ground pepper
1   pound thinly cut pork chops or turkey
       scallopine, cut into 3-by-½-inch strips
2   tablespoons vegetable oil
2   large eggs, beaten
1   bunch green onions or 1 medium onion,
       chopped
1   10-ounce package frozen peas or snow peas

· · ·

In the best
of all worlds,
pork fried rice is
made with leftover
rice. If, however,
you have none,
start cooking the
rice before you
begin stir-frying
the pork.

· · ·

82

Express Lane Cookbook

If using raw rice, bring 3 cups water to a boil in a medium-size saucepan; add rice. Return to a boil, stir, reduce heat to low, cover and cook for 20 minutes, or until tender. If time allows, cover and chill, or use straight from the pan.

Mix 1 tablespoon soy sauce, sugar, cornstarch, salt and pepper in a medium bowl. Add pork or turkey to soy-sauce mixture and stir to combine. Set aside for 20 minutes at room temperature or for up to 24 hours, covered and refrigerated.

Heat 1 tablespoon oil in a wok or large skillet over high heat until very hot. Pour beaten eggs over the bottom of the pan and cook like a pancake until fairly firm; remove from the wok or skillet and set aside. When cool, cut into thin strips about the width of spaghetti.

Add remaining 1 tablespoon oil to the wok or skillet. Heat over high heat until very hot. Add pork or turkey and stir-fry until opaque. Add green onions or chopped onion and cook briefly, about 1 minute. Add peas, cooked rice and remaining 1 teaspoon soy sauce.

Serves 4, with leftovers.

Chicken & Turkey

ROASTED, FRIED, BAKED in casseroles, smothered in tomatoes, or herbed, spiced and stuffed, chicken has replaced ground beef as the affordable, convenient meat of choice. As a main dish, it has become so reliable that the busiest cooks will buy chicken breast an hour before dinner is due on the table without the foggiest notion of what to do with it. Often a meal is planned on the drive home from the supermarket.

Once, chicken was only sold whole and was almost inevitably roasted, usually at 350 degrees—the universal temperature for as long as ovens have had thermostats. Only relatively recently have we had access to so many cuts of chicken—bone-in, boneless, all white, all dark, pieces, whole—and there is no longer a single rule of thumb or cooking temperature that applies to all cuts. Moreover, today's cooks no longer have time to cool their heels while the bird roasts at a moderate temperature.

FORTUNATELY, HOWEVER, today's fryer is neither as old nor as tough as the barnyard hen of long ago. We can jack up the heat and not worry as much about toughening the meat. Because it is tender, chicken takes easily to moist simmering, dry roasting or quick frying.

Though chicken breast offers the most in convenience, it has the least flavor of all the cuts and overcooks in a heartbeat. A boned, skinless chicken breast half can be ready in as little as 10 minutes. Longer, and you'll get dry meat. A good chicken breast has juice that's clear, while the meat is white all the way through. Bone-in chicken takes more time to cook, but it has more flavor and tolerates heat better. A thigh, for instance, might be done in 30 minutes, but won't be overcooked at 40.

When you want to put effort into a side dish, make baked whole chicken. Season it with salt, pepper and a dried herb (I like thyme), and let it bake while you prepare something else. For a complete dinner, add chunked vegetables and potatoes to the baking pan.

Here are some simple favorites to give you a jump-start on the week's menu plan.

chicken & turkey

Sautéed Chicken Breast Sandwiches

• • • • • • • • • • • •

I WALKED INTO OUR COMPANY CAFETERIA one day and noticed that chicken sandwiches were on the menu for $3. It was a concept I had never considered: too easy, I guess.

Don't overlook the obvious. Just because this takes little time or thought to prepare doesn't mean it isn't good.

2	tablespoons olive oil or vegetable oil
2	boneless, skinless chicken breast halves
1	teaspoon dried thyme
½	teaspoon salt
1	teaspoon freshly ground pepper
4	kaiser rolls, poppy seed rolls or 8 pieces of bread
	Lettuce and/or tomatoes (optional)

Heat oil in a large skillet over medium-high heat. Sprinkle chicken breast halves with thyme, salt and pepper. Add to the skillet and sauté, turning chicken frequently, until brown on both sides and cooked through, about 10 minutes.

Slice thinly and pile on rolls, layering with lettuce and tomato slices, if desired.

Serves 4.

Variation

Grilled Chicken Breast Salad: Slice the chicken thinly and fan it out on a bed of romaine and leaf lettuce. Dress with Italian dressing and sprinkle with black olives, then garnish with artichoke hearts.

Quick Chicken Sandwiches

CHICKEN SANDWICHES ARE SIMPLE, nutritious supplements to soup meals when soup just isn't enough. This boneless, skinless chicken breast cooks in just 10 minutes and can feed 4 people when sliced thin and piled on sandwiches. I often serve it during the holidays when my palate tires of rich foods.

½ cup water or chicken broth
2 boneless, skinless chicken breast halves
8 slices good-quality sandwich bread
About 2 tablespoons mayonnaise
Sliced red onion, about ½ medium, (optional)
Sliced peeled cucumber, about ½ medium (optional)

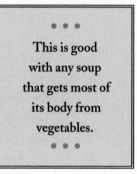

This is good with any soup that gets most of its body from vegetables.

Pour water or broth into a small skillet; bring to a boil over high heat. Add chicken, reduce heat to low, cover and simmer for 10 minutes. Remove from heat and set aside for 5 minutes, still covered.

Remove chicken from broth with a slotted spoon (save broth for soup, if desired). Slice thinly. Spread 4 slices of bread with mayonnaise. Top with a few rings of red onion and 3 thin slices of cucumber, if using. Top with chicken, then a final piece of bread.

Serves 4. ∿ Serve with potato soup.

Asian Chicken

· · · · · · · · · · · · · · · ·

THIS CHICKEN DISH RELIES on blatant exploitation of the palate, hitting taste buds with sweet, salty and sour flavors with a take-no-prisoners attitude. It works. You'll love it. Use any vinegar you have, but aromatic kinds (herbed white vinegar, red wine vinegar or rice wine vinegar) will add flavor. Add minced jalapeño, if you dare.

4	boneless, skinless chicken breast halves
3	tablespoons soy sauce
1½	tablespoons vinegar
2-3	tablespoons light brown sugar
1	garlic clove, finely chopped
¼	teaspoon freshly ground pepper

· · ·

The best-tasting soy sauces are naturally brewed, such as Kikkoman.

· · ·

Preheat the oven to 350 degrees. Lightly oil a glass baking dish large enough to hold chicken breasts in a single layer.

Place chicken breasts in the dish. Combine remaining ingredients and pour over chicken. Bake for 20 minutes, or until chicken is cooked through.

Serve hot or cold.

Serves 4. ∽ Serve with pasta salad and hot rolls.

Greek Chicken

• • • • • • • • • • • • • • • •

YOU CAN'T BE TOO RICH, too thin or have too many chicken breast recipes. Or at least that's the way it feels to most cooks who want to make a fast dinner that is tasty and fairly low in fat.

This recipe borrows from Greek cuisine, combining garlic, oregano and lemons, which boost the unassertive flavor of the chicken. The recipe calls for lots of rice.

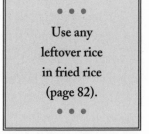

3	cups water
1-1½	cups raw long-grain white rice
4	boneless, skinless chicken breast halves
	Juice of 2 lemons
1-2	teaspoons dried oregano
1	teaspoon freshly ground pepper, or to taste
	Salt to taste
1	garlic clove, minced
2	tablespoons olive oil

• • •

Use any
leftover rice
in fried rice
(page 82).

• • •

Bring water to boil in a medium saucepan; add rice. Return to a boil, stir, cover and simmer for 20 minutes, or until tender.

Meanwhile, cut chicken breasts into 3-by-½-inch strips. Sprinkle with lemon juice, oregano, pepper and salt; set aside.

About 5 minutes before rice is completely cooked, heat oil over medium-high heat in a large skillet. When it is hot, add garlic and chicken and cook, stirring, until chicken is opaque and just beginning to brown, about 5 minutes.

Serves 4. ∽ Serve over or with hot rice, with sliced fresh tomatoes sprinkled with pepper and crumbled feta cheese.

Orange-Ginger Chicken

· ·

MANY COOKS THINK THAT MARINATED FOODS must be started early in the day. If they're too busy to do it then, they think it's not an option at night.

Don't forgo this Chinese-flavored chicken because you got a late start on dinner preparation; marinating it while the grill heats is sufficient.

½	cup soy sauce
2	tablespoons olive oil or vegetable oil
2	tablespoons grated fresh ginger
1	garlic clove, minced
1	tablespoon grated orange or tangerine zest (orange part of rind only)
2½ -3	pounds chicken, cut into serving pieces

> · · ·
>
> Don't worry about peeling the ginger. You won't notice the peel in the finished dish.
>
> · · ·

Mix soy sauce, oil, ginger, garlic and orange or tangerine zest in a large bowl.

Place chicken in the bowl; toss to coat.

Preheat the broiler or a grill, with a rack 6 inches from the heat source.

If broiling, place chicken in a shallow roasting pan. Broil or grill for 15 minutes per side, basting often with extra soy-sauce mixture, until the insides lose any traces of pink. Dark meat takes a litle longer; if the meat browns too quickly, turn it often. Serve at once.

Serves 4 to 6. ∾ Serve with cooked rice and a green vegetable, such as Brussels sprouts or peas.

Italian Chicken Salad

· ·

CHICKEN SALAD IS MADE with mayonnaise and celery, right? Not necessarily. It is a dish of multiple personalities. This vinaigrette-and-vegetable version, inspired by the flavors of Italy, makes a really quick dinner, going together as fast as the ingredients can be assembled. Serve on a bed of lettuce, if desired.

· · ·

One chicken breast half takes about 2 minutes to cook in the microwave.

· · ·

4	skinless, boneless chicken breast halves
3	tablespoons olive oil
1	cup walnuts, coarsely chopped
1-2	red peppers, cored and cut into 1-inch pieces
1	6-ounce jar marinated artichoke hearts
½-1	cup fresh or frozen peas
1	teaspoon dried oregano
	Juice of 1 lemon
	Salt and freshly ground pepper to taste
2-3	green onions, trimmed and diced

To microwave chicken breast: Place chicken on a plate and cover with wax paper. Microwave on high power for 8 to 9 minutes, rearranging twice during cooking.

To cook on the stovetop: In a large skillet, bring ½ inch of water to a boil. Add chicken breasts and return to a boil over high heat. Cover, reduce heat to low and simmer, turning the chicken after 5 minutes, until only the faintest hint of pink remains in the meat, about 10 minutes. (Cut into it to check for doneness; you'll be cutting it into pieces later anyway.) Cool.

Meanwhile, heat oil in a large skillet over medium-high heat. Add walnuts and stir over high heat for 1 to 2 minutes; watch carefully so they don't burn. Add peppers and stir.

Drain juice from the artichoke jar into the skillet. Chop artichoke hearts into 2 or 3 pieces and add to the skillet with peas and oregano; cook for 3 more minutes, stirring.

Transfer to a large bowl. Add lemon juice and season generously with salt and pepper. Pull chicken apart with your fingers or cut it into chunks; add to the bowl and mix. Sprinkle green onions over salad. Serve warm or cold.

Serves 4 to 6. ∾ **Serve with rolls and fresh fruit, such as cantaloupe or watermelon.**

chicken & turkey

Parslied Chicken Bake

• •

FRYING CHICKEN IS TIME-CONSUMING and messy, but boy, does it taste good. Some of us who have eliminated fried chicken from our diets because of concerns about fat get our fix of crispy skin by baking bread-crumb-coated chicken at a high temperature in the oven. Any extra bread crumbs will be easier to dispose of than the several cups of hot grease that you'd have after frying.

Removing the skin from the bird is the most healthful way to eat it, but not always the most satisfying. If you prefer chicken with the skin on, leave it on in this recipe.

¾	cup fine, dry bread crumbs
3	tablespoons chopped fresh parsley
2	tablespoons grated Parmesan cheese
½	garlic clove, minced
¼	teaspoon salt
¼	teaspoon freshly ground pepper
2½-3	pounds chicken, cut into serving pieces, skinned, if desired

• • •

If using boneless chicken breast, proceed as directed but bake for only 15 minutes.

• • •

Preheat the oven to 400 degrees. Lightly oil a large cookie sheet.

Combine bread crumbs, parsley, Parmesan, garlic, salt and pepper in a plastic bag; shake to mix. Place 2 pieces of chicken in the bag and shake to coat. Place chicken pieces on the cookie sheet; repeat with remaining chicken pieces.

Bake chicken for 40 minutes (breasts should take no more than 30 minutes), turning once halfway through. The outsides will be lightly browned and the insides will have lost all traces of pink.

Serves 4. ∾ Serve with rolls, lima beans and cooked carrots sprinkled with dill.

Deviled Chicken Breasts

● ●

IN CULINARY TERMS, something that's deviled is usually flavored with tangy mustard and always starts a slow burn on the palate. In this deviled chicken, the flavor comes from spices, not fat.

1	teaspoon chili powder
½	teaspoon dry mustard
½	teaspoon salt, or to taste
2	tablespoons water
1	tablespoon vinegar (any kind)
¼	teaspoon Tabasco or other hot pepper sauce
	Dash of Worcestershire sauce
4	boneless, skinless chicken breast halves

> ● ● ●
>
> You can substitute cut-up chicken parts for the breasts, but cook them a little longer.
>
> ● ● ●

Preheat the broiler or grill, with a rack 6 inches from the heat source. Lightly oil the broiler pan or grill.

Combine spices in a large bowl. Stir in water, vinegar, Tabasco or hot pepper sauce and Worcestershire sauce. Add chicken and turn to coat it with spices.

Broil or grill chicken for 5 minutes. Turn and baste with marinade. Cook for 10 minutes more, or until the insides lose all traces of pink.

Serves 4. ∽ Serve with boiled potatoes and sliced tomatoes
or with cauliflower and green noodles.

Fast Chicken Fajitas

F AJITAS ARE TO TEX-MEX COOKING what stir-fry is to Chinese. To hassled American cooks, both kinds of dishes are a fast way to put a good-tasting dinner on the table. In these fajitas, the vegetables are complemented by a little chicken breast, cheese and sour cream and then rolled into tortillas—much like a burrito, but messier. The vegetables are best when they still have a little crunch to them.

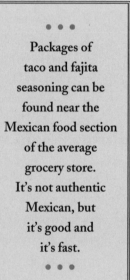

3   tablespoons vegetable oil
1   medium onion, sliced and separated into
       rings
2   boneless, skinless chicken breast halves, cut
       into strips
1   tablespoon taco or fajita seasoning
1   4-ounce can whole mild green chilies, cut
       into strips
8   6-inch flour tortillas
1   8-ounce container sour cream (nonfat will
       work)
    About ½ pound Cheddar cheese, shredded
    About ½ cup chunky Mexican salsa
1   medium tomato, cored and cut into strips

• • •
Packages of
taco and fajita
seasoning can be
found near the
Mexican food section
of the average
grocery store.
It's not authentic
Mexican, but
it's good and
it's fast.
• • •

Heat oil over high heat in a large skillet; add onion and chicken. Stir-fry until onion softens a little and chicken turns opaque, about 2 minutes. After about 1 minute, stir in taco or fajita seasoning.

Add green chilies, reduce heat to low, cover and cook for 5 minutes.

Heat tortillas until warm and flexible. You can do this over a gas flame, in a dry skillet or in a microwave. (To heat over a gas flame, lay 1 tortilla directly on the burner and turn every 2 seconds with tongs until warm and just beginning to get brown spots. Or heat a skillet on high heat, and heat 1 tortilla at a time, turning until pliable and warm, about 10 to 15 seconds. To microwave, wrap tortillas in a damp cloth towel and microwave on medium power for about 1 minute. Change the position of tortillas in the stack, moving those inside to the outside, and microwave for 30 seconds.)

Spread each tortilla with a stripe of sour cream across its diameter, then sprinkle with a little cheese; add chicken mixture. Top with salsa and tomato. Fold the tortilla over the filling and serve.

Serves 4. ∿ **Serve with sliced strawberries or fresh chunked pineapple.**

High-Spice Chicken

● ● ● ● ● ● ● ● ● ● ● ● ● ● ● ● ● ● ● ●

S PICE RUBS ARE MORE POPULAR than ever, probably because so many low-fat meats need help in the flavor department. Chicken breast is no exception: it improves greatly when rubbed with a combination of herbs and spices.

The following mixture is not too hot. It may seem weird to include sugar in the mix, but it serves to round out the spices in your mouth.

2	tablespoons ground cumin
1	tablespoon paprika
1	tablespoon chili powder
1	tablespoon dried oregano
2	teaspoons light brown sugar
1	teaspoon freshly ground pepper
1	teaspoon salt
2½-3	pounds chicken, cut into serving pieces, skinned if desired

● ● ●

This will seem
like a lot of spices.
Use them all.

● ● ●

Preheat the oven to 375 degrees. Lightly oil a cookie sheet.

Combine all seasonings on a large plate. Rub seasonings over chicken and place chicken on the cookie sheet.

Bake for about 15 minutes for boneless chicken breasts, 35 to 45 minutes for dark meat, or until juices run clear when meat is pierced with a knife.

Serve immediately.

Serves 4 to 6. ∾ Serve with fresh corn and tomatoes
in the summer or with sweet potatoes in the fall.

Easy Pepper Chicken

· ·

I THINK SPICE RUBS IMPROVE virtually all meats, and the variety of seasonings is endless. The following mixture relies on the heat of pepper. You wouldn't call it subtle, but it's not as "in-your-face" as the previous recipe. It's also less work. I like it because I usually have all the ingredients at home, so I can have a good dinner without shopping.

1   tablespoon paprika
½   teaspoon freshly ground pepper
½   teaspoon cayenne pepper
½   teaspoon salt
4   boneless, skinless chicken breast halves
2   tablespoons olive oil

· · ·

Cook extra chicken breast because leftovers can be sliced for sandwiches.

· · ·

Combine seasonings and sprinkle evenly over chicken.

Heat oil in a large skillet over medium-high heat. Brown chicken for 2 minutes on each side.

Reduce heat to medium, cover skillet and cook until chicken is done, about 10 minutes, or until the insides have lost all traces of pink.

Serves 4.   ∾   Serve with baked or boiled potatoes and green beans.

Chicken Noodles

· ·

Sauce has been called the soul of a dish. But if you're short on time, does that mean you're doomed to wander culinary purgatory, doomed to sauceless meals?

Not necessarily. Sauces don't have to be time-consuming, fattening, butter-laden béarnaises and hollandaises. A sauce can be created by simply using broth or wine to scrape up the bits of browned meat from the bottom of the skillet.

½-¾   pound spaghetti or other thin noodles
3   tablespoons olive oil
2   boneless, skinless chicken breasts,
       sliced into 3-by-½-inch strips
3   garlic cloves, minced
¼   pound mushrooms, cleaned and sliced
       Juice of 1 lemon
1   14-to-16-ounce can chicken broth
       (about 2 cups)
¼   cup minced fresh parsley, or more to taste
       Salt and freshly ground pepper
       Grated Parmesan cheese (optional)

In a large pot of boiling, salted water, cook spaghetti or other noodles for about 8 minutes, or until strands are cooked through but slightly firm.

Meanwhile, in a large skillet, heat oil over high heat and add chicken. Cook, stirring constantly, for 2 to 3 minutes, until chicken is opaque. Transfer with a slotted spoon to a large plate.

Add garlic to the skillet and sauté for 1 minute, stirring. Add mushrooms and sauté, stirring. After a minute or so, add lemon juice, chicken broth and parsley. Boil to reduce the liquid by about half; add chicken and heat through. Season with salt and pepper to taste.

Serve over drained noodles, sprinkled with Parmesan cheese, if desired.

Serves 3 to 4. ∾ **Serve with broccoli or Brussels sprouts.**

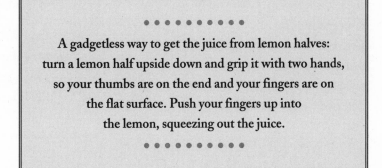

• • • • • • • • • • •

A gadgetless way to get the juice from lemon halves:
turn a lemon half upside down and grip it with two hands,
so your thumbs are on the end and your fingers are on
the flat surface. Push your fingers up into
the lemon, squeezing out the juice.

• • • • • • • • • •

Tomato-Thyme Chicken

• •

Canned tomato sauce is the ultimate convenience product. Combined with an herb or two, it makes a tasty low-fat sauce for chicken, fish or baked pork chops.

1 tablespoon olive oil
4 boneless, skinless chicken breast halves
1 8-ounce can tomato sauce
1 teaspoon dried thyme
 Salt and freshly ground pepper to taste

• • •
Lots of
freshly ground
pepper enhances
this dish.
• • •

Heat oil in a large skillet over medium-high heat. Add chicken breasts and cook for 2 minutes on each side.

Pour tomato sauce over chicken; sprinkle with thyme. Cover and cook for 10 to 15 minutes, or until the insides have lost all traces of pink. Season with salt and pepper.

Serves 4. ∾ Serve with roasted carrots and rice.

Honey Chicken

· · · · · · · · · · · · · · · · · ·

SWEET INGREDIENTS AND SALTY ONES have been combined for centuries to heighten the flavor of foods. Asian cuisines, in particular, often balance the two, sometimes adding the tastes of sour and hot. This quick chicken dish is nicely balanced and low in fat.

3   tablespoons soy sauce
2   tablespoons honey
1   teaspoon vegetable oil
4   chicken breast halves, bone-in or boneless

Preheat the oven to 400 degrees, or preheat the broiler or grill, with a rack 4 inches from the heat source. Lightly oil the broiler pan or grill.

Combine soy sauce, honey and oil in a small dish or pan. Heat in a microwave or on top of the stove, stirring, until honey dissolves.

Brush honey mixture on chicken and bake for 20 to 30 minutes for a bone-in breast, or for as little as 10 minutes for a boneless chicken breast half. Or grill or broil for about 20 minutes, turning occasionally so chicken doesn't burn. Brush with honey sauce during the last 10 minutes of cooking. Serve immediately.

Serves 4. ∿ **Serve with corn on the cob,
sliced tomatoes and hot rolls or with rice and broccoli.**

Quick Chicken Curry

∙ ∙

COMMERCIAL CURRY POWDER is a tasty but rather one-dimensional seasoning. This simple homemade curry powder is multileveled in flavor and does wonders for chicken.

1	tablespoon vegetable oil
½	cup chopped green onions or ordinary onion
2	garlic cloves, minced
1	tablespoon ground coriander
1	teaspoon ground cumin
½	teaspoon salt
¼	teaspoon ground turmeric
1	28-ounce can tomatoes
4	boneless, skinless chicken breast halves

> ∙ ∙ ∙
>
> You can substitute 1 pound of turkey scallopine for chicken. Begin the rice immediately after you start cooking the onions and garlic.
>
> ∙ ∙ ∙

Heat oil in a large skillet over medium heat; add green onions or onion and cook until softened, about 15 minutes. Add spices and cook, stirring, for 1 to 2 minutes.

Add tomatoes, chopping them into small pieces as you add them, along with their juice. Simmer, uncovered, for 5 minutes.

Add chicken breasts, cover and simmer for 15 minutes, or until the insides have lost all traces of pink. Serve with tomato sauce spooned over top.

Serves 4. ∽ Serve with hot rice and steamed green beans.

Roast Chicken

· · · · · · · · · · · · · · · ·

Simplicity is the beauty of roast chicken, and it should not be underestimated. Roast chicken invites no basting, no watching, no fuss. And whole chickens are some of the best bargains at the meat counter. Besides, roast chicken tastes great and makes the house smell wonderful.

The secret to a quick roasting is high temperatures that sear the outside of the bird, crisping the skin but keeping the meat moist. Whenever I roast a chicken, I preheat the oven to 450 degrees the minute I walk in the door, put the chicken on a roasting pan and wash some baking potatoes.

Then I put them all in the oven and go about my business. About 30 minutes later, I reduce the heat to 400 degrees and cook for another 15 to 20 minutes.

If, after cooking, the thigh meat still looks a little pink where it joins the bird, I carve both leg quarters off, return them to the roasting pan, skin side up, and put them back in the oven for 5 minutes while I slice the breast meat.

1   4-to-5-pound chicken
Salt
Freshly ground pepper

Preheat the oven to 450 degrees.

Remove giblets from cavity and rinse chicken inside and out. Set chicken on a rack in a roasting pan with shallow sides (no higher than 1 inch); sprinkle with salt and pepper. Place in the oven and bake for 30 minutes; reduce heat to 400 degrees. Bake for 15 to 25 minutes more, or until thigh juices run clear when poked with a fork.

Remove from oven. Let stand for 10 minutes before carving to make slicing easier.

Serves 4 to 6. ~ **Serve with baked potatoes and salad.**

Chicken with Mushrooms

• •

Stews are rarely found on the menus of busy cooks since most recipes call for pieces of tough meat that need long, slow simmering.

Chicken on the bone, however, is fairly tender meat that makes a great stew, even if you don't have lots of time to spend in the kitchen. This stew can be completed in less than 45 minutes and is especially good for company.

4	tablespoons olive oil
½	pound fresh mushrooms, trimmed and cleaned; quartered, if large
3½-4	pounds chicken, cut into 8 serving pieces
2	medium onions, sliced
¼	cup all-purpose flour
1	14-to-16 ounce can (about 2 cups) beef broth
1	teaspoon dried thyme
1	28-ounce can tomatoes, drained (reserve juice)
¼	cup stuffed green olives, rinsed
	Salt and freshly ground pepper to taste

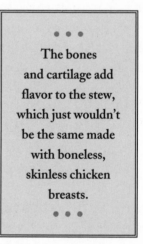

• • •

The bones and cartilage add flavor to the stew, which just wouldn't be the same made with boneless, skinless chicken breasts.

• • •

In a Dutch oven or large skillet, heat 2 tablespoons oil over high heat. Add mushrooms and toss until they are glazed and beginning to brown, about 3 minutes. Transfer with a slotted spoon to a plate; set aside.

Add remaining 2 tablespoons oil to the skillet and brown chicken on all sides on high heat so it browns quickly, about 10 minutes. Turn chicken often if you are worried it will burn, but you're aiming for a rich brown color. Add onions, reduce heat to medium-high and cook, stirring, for about 3 minutes. Stir in flour and cook for about 3 minutes. Add beef broth, thyme and tomatoes, chopping or crushing them through your fingers as you add them, stirring to combine. Reduce heat to medium-low and simmer for 10 minutes.

Add olives and simmer for 10 to 20 minutes more, so the flavors meld.

If sauce is too thin, remove chicken to a serving platter or plates and boil sauce rapidly to the desired consistency. If it is too thick, add tomato juice, water or more beef broth. Before serving, stir in mushrooms and salt and pepper.

Serves 4 to 6. ∾ **Serve with hot rice and snow peas.**

Pretty-in-Pink Chicken

●●●●●●●●●●●●●●●●●●●●●●●●●●●●●●●

A KETCHUP-SPIKED DRESSING makes this chicken delicious and pretty, especially when the chicken is grilled. It's a perfect dish for summer entertaining and one of my most popular recipes.

Because I think of this as a "party recipe," I've always made it with whole chicken breasts. That's a hefty portion, however, and if you want less meat, substitute chicken breast halves.

Salad

- 4 boneless, skinless chicken breasts
   Salt and freshly ground pepper
- 4 small heads Bibb lettuce or 2 heads
   Butterhead lettuce, washed and dried
- 2 ripe beefsteak or plum tomatoes
   (or about 16 cherry tomatoes), sliced
- 2 ounces feta or blue cheese
   (about ⅓-½ cup crumbled)

Dressing

- 1 egg yolk
- ½ cup plus 1 tablespoon red wine vinegar
- 6 tablespoons sugar
- 2½ cups vegetable oil
- 2-3 tablespoons ketchup
- 1 tablespoon poppy seeds

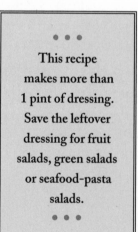

● ● ●

This recipe makes more than 1 pint of dressing. Save the leftover dressing for fruit salads, green salads or seafood-pasta salads.

● ● ●

To make salad: Preheat the grill or broiler, with a rack 4 inches from the heat source. Generously oil the grill or broiler pan.

Pound chicken breasts with the side of a saucer or with a mallet until they are about ½ inch thick; season with salt and pepper. Grill or broil for 3 minutes on each side, or until insides lose all traces of pink. Set aside and keep warm.

Line plates generously with lettuce. Place tomatoes on one side of the plate. Crumble a little cheese over the top of them.

To make dressing: Combine egg yolk, vinegar and sugar in a blender or bowl and blend or whisk rapidly to combine. Drizzle in oil and continue blending or whisking; beat in ketchup and poppy seeds.

Place warm or hot chicken breast on top of lettuce and cheese. Drizzle with dressing and serve.

Serves 4. ∾ **Serve with hot rolls or homemade corn bread.**

Glazed Chicken Thighs

• •

THIS DISH MADE WITH CHICKEN THIGHS is a poor-man's barbecue with a sweet-pungent flavor. It's a good dish for cooks who like to plan ahead because you can combine all the ingredients and refrigerate it overnight or longer so it's ready to slip in the oven anytime without last-minute worries.

I like to take this dish to new mothers because it cooks easily, reheats well and contains no onions or garlic to upset the tummy of a nursing baby. It would also be a good dish to bring to new neighbors, sick friends or any other potluck occasion.

2½	pounds chicken thighs, skinned
⅓	cup molasses
3	tablespoons vinegar, preferably apple cider vinegar
1	tablespoon Worcestershire sauce
1	tablespoon Dijon-style mustard
½	teaspoon Tabasco or other hot sauce (optional)
1	teaspoon freshly ground pepper
½	teaspoon salt

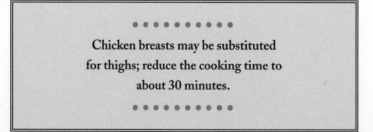

• • • • • • • • •

Chicken breasts may be substituted
for thighs; reduce the cooking time to
about 30 minutes.

• • • • • • • • •

Preheat the oven to 375 degrees.

Place chicken in a 9-by-13-inch baking dish or a shallow, wide casserole dish large enough to hold chicken in a single layer.

Combine molasses, vinegar, Worcestershire sauce, mustard, Tabasco or other hot sauce (if using), pepper and salt in a small bowl and stir until evenly mixed.

Pour over chicken and bake for 45 minutes, or until inside of chicken has lost all traces of pink. Serve immediately.

Serves 6. ∾ **Serve with buttered noodles and green beans.**

Chicken-Cheese Tortillas

· ·

A FLOUR TORTILLA IS THE PERFECT VEHICLE for disguising leftovers. Shredded cold chicken can be combined with cheese and chilies for a delicious dinner, but if you don't have leftovers, use uncooked chicken breasts.

3	tablespoons olive oil
1	medium onion, diced
1	large garlic clove, minced
4	boneless, skinless chicken breast halves
1	4-ounce can chopped mild green chilies
1	jalapeño pepper, seeded and minced (optional)
½	teaspoon ground cumin
	Salt to taste (about ½ teaspoon)
10	8-inch flour tortillas
2	cups grated Monterey Jack cheese

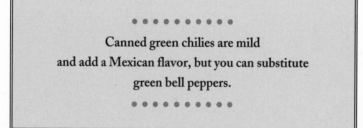

· · · · · · · · · · ·

Canned green chilies are mild
and add a Mexican flavor, but you can substitute
green bell peppers.

· · · · · · · · · · ·

Heat oil over medium-high heat in a large skillet. Add onion and garlic and cook, stirring occasionally, for 7 to 10 minutes, until onion begins to color.

Meanwhile, cut chicken into small cubes. Add chicken, green chilies and jalapeño pepper, if using, to the skillet. Sprinkle with cumin; increase the heat to high. Cook, stirring constantly, until chicken is opaque, about 1 to 2 minutes. Taste and add salt if necessary; remove from the heat.

Preheat the oven to 300 degrees. Warm tortillas over a gas flame, in a skillet or in a microwave (see page 97). Oil a 9-by-13-inch baking dish.

Divide chicken filling equally among tortillas, spooning filling down the center of each tortilla; top with cheese. Roll up to enclose filling; place in the oiled baking dish, seam side down.

Cover the baking dish with foil or a lid and bake until tortillas are heated through and cheese is melted, about 10 minutes.

Serves 4. ∿ Serve with heated canned pinto beans and
a salad of grapefruit sections and avocado.

Turkey Burgers with Tarragon Mustard

. . . .

TO MY PALATE, ground turkey is no substitute for ground beef, and whoever tries to persuade me otherwise is wrong. Especially when you can get extra-lean ground beef, there seems little reason to substitute ground turkey to save a few fat grams. On the other hand, there are times—as in this recipe—when ground turkey is just what will taste best. Here it benefits from the association with tarragon and mustard.

2 pounds ground turkey
2 tablespoons olive oil
2 teaspoons red wine vinegar
1 tablespoon Dijon-style mustard
1 teaspoon dried tarragon
  Salt and freshly ground pepper

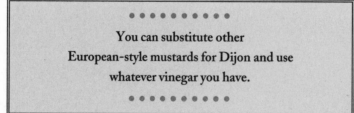

. . . .

You can substitute other
European-style mustards for Dijon and use
whatever vinegar you have.

. . . .

Preheat oven to 475 degrees. Lightly oil a broiler pan or cookie sheet.

Form ground turkey into 6 or 8 patties; the mixture will be softer than ground beef. Place patties on the pan or cookie sheet.

Whisk together remaining ingredients; spoon a little over each patty.

Bake for 10 minutes, turn patties and spoon 1 teaspoon mustard mixture over each. The patties should be cooked through; if they are not, cook for 2 minutes more.

Serves 4 to 6. ∽ **Serve with rice or thin noodles and broccoli.**

Turkey Meatballs and Spaghetti

· · · · · · · · · · · · · · · ·

MAKING MEATBALLS ISN'T AS FAST as broiling a burger, but it sure doesn't take all afternoon. The first time you do it will be the slowest; after that, you can do it with your eyes closed. In this recipe, the meatballs are baked rather than pan-fried, making them less messy and lower in fat. You can walk away and get other things done while they bake, rather than having to watch and turn them constantly.

1   large egg
3   slices white bread, crusts removed
     Water or milk to soak bread
½   cup grated Parmesan cheese
2   tablespoons chopped fresh parsley
1   large garlic clove, minced
½   teaspoon salt
½   teaspoon freshly ground pepper
1   pound lean ground turkey or lean ground
     beef
4   cups prepared spaghetti sauce (or one 32-
     ounce jar)

Preheat the oven to 375 degrees. Lightly oil a cookie sheet.

Lightly beat egg in a large bowl. In a separate bowl, dip bread into water or milk to dampen; firmly squeeze out excess liquid. Break up bread and beat into egg with a fork.

Stir in cheese, parsley, garlic, salt and pepper; gently mix in turkey or beef. Form into balls the size of walnuts.

Place meatballs on the cookie sheet and bake for 15 minutes, or until cooked through.

Meanwhile, heat spaghetti sauce in a large saucepan or skillet over low heat. When meatballs are done, gently stir them into sauce. Extra meatballs can be frozen; meatballs in sauce can also be frozen.

Makes about 16 meatballs; serves 4 generously. ∿ **Serve over long noodles, such as vermicelli or spaghetti, accompanied by broccoli or green beans.**

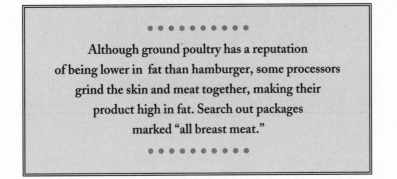

· · · · · · · · · ·

Although ground poultry has a reputation of being lower in fat than hamburger, some processors grind the skin and meat together, making their product high in fat. Search out packages marked "all breast meat."

· · · · · · · · · ·

Fish & Seafood

· ·

FOR THE COOK EAGER to get dinner on the table, fish is a natural. It's faster to prepare than nearly any other food, high in vitamins and minerals, and lean. What fat it does have is actually good for us.

Choosing fresh fish is the hardest part of cooking it. If it smells fresh, it is. If it smells like fish, it will taste fishy. Cooks who live on a coastline or in a major metropolitan area generally have unlimited access to per-fectly fresh fish. I don't. When I want a wide variety of good seafood, I have to go to a specialty shop, which is neither nearby nor particularly affordable. It's something I do only on special occasions.

That doesn't mean I don't eat fish, though. Several types of fish are dependably fresh at the supermarket. Catfish and trout are farm-raised, often close to home, and are usually fresh. Sometimes frozen fish is the wisest purchase. Orange roughy is flash-

frozen on fishing boats, preserving flavor and texture. Shrimp is virtually always frozen before it reaches the stores and therefore retains its flavor. And every so often, my local supermarket features a certain fish—usually salmon—at a special price, which ensures rapid turnover and good quality.

Impeccably fresh fish doesn't need much done to it. Sometimes I spread broiled fish with a thin coating of mayonnaise, which, with its high oil content and subtle seasoning, is the perfect "basting." Or I brush it with butter, or butter seasoned with a hint of herbs, or olive oil flavored with garlic.

OVERCOOKING FISH IS EASY—and nothing destroys fish like overcooking. Though there are exceptions, most fish should be cooked for about 10 minutes per inch of thickness; watch carefully. If the fillet tapers at the end, even it up by folding the tail under to double the thickness. Remember that the presence of bones will increase cooking time.

The following recipes, which feature simple preparations of farmed, previously frozen and canned fish, show that even the constraints of the supermarket fish counter need not cramp a cook's style.

fish & seafood

Linguine with Clams

· ·

FOR THIS DISH TO TASTE GOOD, it must have fresh parsley and fresh lemon juice. Please don't substitute dried or bottled.

¾ pound linguine or other long, thin noodles

6 tablespoons olive oil

3 garlic cloves, minced

¾ cup finely chopped fresh parsley

1 6½-ounce can minced clams with liquid
Juice and grated zest (yellow part of rind only) from 1 lemon

½ teaspoon salt, or to taste
Grated Parmesan cheese (optional)

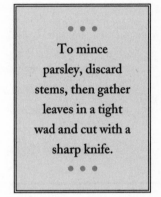

· · ·

To mince parsley, discard stems, then gather leaves in a tight wad and cut with a sharp knife.

· · ·

In a large pot of boiling, salted water, cook noodles until barely tender, about 10 minutes. Meanwhile, heat oil over low heat in a medium skillet. Add garlic and cook for 5 minutes, or until softened. Add parsley to the skillet, then clams, lemon juice, zest and salt. Heat just until bubbling and serve over hot, drained noodles.

Pass cheese at the table for topping, if desired.

Serves 3 to 4. ∼ **Serve with steamed broccoli and whole-grain rolls (page 187).**

Shrimp and Feta Sauce

· ·

SURVEYS SHOW THAT FEW COOKS have feta cheese in the fridge, and only a few more would go out and buy it if a recipe called for it. Too bad, because the earthy saltiness of feta cheese makes it go well with lots of foods—pasta, potatoes, fresh vegetables, salads . . . I love feta cheese in just about anything. It is a wonderful complement to shrimp and tomatoes in this Greek-inspired dish.

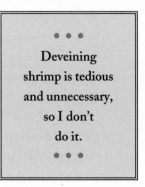

· · ·

Deveining
shrimp is tedious
and unnecessary,
so I don't
do it.

· · ·

2   tablespoons olive oil or vegetable oil
4   garlic cloves (or more to taste), minced
2   14-ounce cans stewed tomatoes
2   tablespoons chopped parsley,
       preferably fresh
1   teaspoon dried oregano
    Salt and freshly ground pepper to taste
1   pound uncooked shrimp, peeled
⅓   cup crumbled feta cheese (about 2 ounces)

Heat oil over medium-high heat in a large skillet. Add garlic and cook until just beginning to brown. Add tomatoes, parsley, oregano, salt and pepper, reduce heat to low and let sauce simmer.

When sauce has thickened to desired consistency (about 20 minutes), add shrimp and feta cheese. Cook until shrimp are pink, about 5 minutes.

Serves 4.   ∽   Serve over cooked rice or pasta with a side dish of peas or green beans.

Spicy Orange Shrimp

· ·

DESCRIBED TO ME OVER THE PHONE BY A FRIEND who raved about it, this dish requires just a few ingredients and very little time to prepare.

· · ·

To cut the
expense, serve
small helpings of
shrimp over
lots of rice.

· · ·

1	tablespoon vegetable oil
2	garlic cloves, minced
1	pound uncooked shrimp, peeled
1½	cups orange juice
1-2	teaspoons Tabasco or other hot pepper sauce, or to taste
2	teaspoons Worcestershire sauce
2	teaspoons light brown sugar
¼	teaspoon salt
1	tablespoon cornstarch, stirred into 1 tablespoon cold water
4	cups cooked long-grain white rice (from 2 cups raw)

Heat oil in a heavy skillet over medium-high heat. Add garlic and cook for 1 minute. Add shrimp and cook until opaque and pink, about 2 minutes.

Stir in orange juice, Tabasco or other hot sauce, Worcestershire sauce, brown sugar and salt. Bring to a boil and boil for 2 minutes. Stir in the dissolved cornstarch. Continue cooking, stirring, until thickened, about 2 to 3 minutes.

Serve immediately over rice.

Serves 4. ∿ Serve with steamed green vegetables,
such as broccoli, snow peas or Brussels sprouts.

Creamy Shrimp Linguine

· ·

THIS CREAMY SHRIMP DISH is a cinch to make and delicious, even if it isn't covered with a fatty sauce.

¾	pound linguine or spaghetti
2	tablespoons olive oil
¼	cup sliced green onions
¼	cup fresh parsley, chopped
2	garlic cloves, minced
½	teaspoon dried basil or 2 teaspoons minced fresh
¼	teaspoon freshly ground pepper
1	cup chicken broth (canned is fine)
1	15-ounce container ricotta cheese
1	pound uncooked shrimp, peeled
	Salt to taste
	Grated Parmesan cheese

In a large pot of boiling, salted water, cook noodles for 10 minutes, or until barely tender; drain. Meanwhile, heat oil in a large skillet over medium-low heat. Add green onions, parsley, garlic, basil and pepper. Cook, stirring, until onions are soft.

Add chicken broth and boil until reduced by half. Add ricotta cheese, stirring to break up lumps. Add shrimp and cook for 10 minutes, until shrimp are pink. Season to taste with salt.

Serve over hot noodles. Top with Parmesan cheese.

Serves 4. ∾ Serve with hot asparagus, peas or broccoli.

Variation

Clam Linguine: Substitute one 6½-ounce can of drained, chopped clams for the shrimp. Heat only long enough for the clams to become hot.

Gingered Scallops

. . . .

CHINESE COOKING BRINGS OUT THE BEST in so many foods, adding loads of flavor but keeping them low in calories.

The following recipe borrows a little flavor from the Chinese, but doesn't require hard-to-find ingredients.

1¼ pounds scallops

3 green onions, trimmed and sliced on the diagonal

2 tablespoons grated ginger

3 tablespoons freshly squeezed lemon juice

2 tablespoons vegetable oil

2 teaspoons honey

2 cups cooked hot rice (from 1 cup raw long-grain white rice)

Place scallops in a lightly oiled baking dish large enough to hold them in a single layer. Combine green onions, ginger, lemon juice, oil and honey in a small bowl. Pour over scallops; set aside while you cook rice.

Preheat the broiler, with the rack 3 to 4 inches from the heat source.

Drain scallops, saving marinade, and broil for about 5 minutes (depending on their size), or until they just lose their translucency and become opaque on the outside. (Little bay scallops may take just 1 minute to cook.) Meanwhile, heat marinade in a small saucepan.

Serve scallops over hot rice, spooning a little marinade over them, if desired.

Serves 4. ❧ Serve with snow peas, peas or green beans.

Southern "Fried" Catfish

● ●

FRYING FISH IS MESSY AND FATTENING, and it's a drag trying to dispose of the oil once you're finished. Oven-frying is quicker, neater and better for the waistline. You can oven-fry many types of fish. Catfish is especially appropriate because its moist meat can stand up to high oven temperatures and because it is farm-raised in clean waters.

- ¾ cup yellow or white cornmeal
- ¼ cup all-purpose flour
- 2 teaspoons salt
- 1 teaspoon cayenne pepper
- 4 serving-size catfish fillets, each about 6 ounces
- 2 tablespoons vegetable oil

Preheat the oven to 400 degrees. Lightly oil a cookie sheet.

Combine dry ingredients in a large, shallow plate and stir to blend. Coat fillets on both sides with cornmeal mixture.

Place fish on the cookie sheet, leaving plenty of room between fillets. Bake for up to 10 minutes, or until fish is opaque throughout.

Serves 4. ∾ Serve with rice and steamed asparagus, peas or another vegetable of choice.

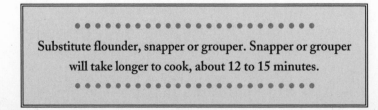

Substitute flounder, snapper or grouper. Snapper or grouper will take longer to cook, about 12 to 15 minutes.

fish & seafood

Dijon Snapper

· · · · · · · · · · · · ·

IF YOU'VE NEVER GRILLED FISH OVER CHARCOAL, you are in for a treat. The slight smokiness contributed by the coals does as much for fish as it does for steak, and perhaps more.

    2   tablespoons Dijon-style mustard
    2   tablespoons wine vinegar
    2   tablespoons honey
    1½ pounds snapper fillets or any firm,
           white fish, or salmon

Preheat the grill or broiler, with a rack about 4 inches from the heat source. Lightly oil the grill or broiler pan.

Combine mustard, vinegar and honey in a small bowl; brush mixture on fish.

Grill fish for 3 to 5 minutes per side, turning once and brushing with sauce, or broil for 4 to 6 minutes, until fish is opaque throughout.

Serves 4. ∾ Serve with potatoes and sliced tomatoes
or with broiled rice and sautéed mushrooms.

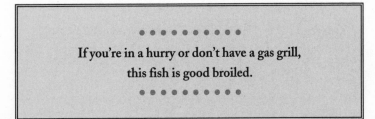

· · · · · · · · · ·

If you're in a hurry or don't have a gas grill,
this fish is good broiled.

· · · · · · · · · ·

Curried Roughy

· ·

ORANGE ROUGHY IS CAUGHT FAR OUT AT SEA and is virtually always flash-frozen on board ship when it is only hours old, so it is usually of high quality.

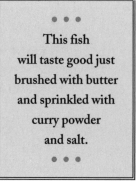

· · ·

This fish
will taste good just
brushed with butter
and sprinkled with
curry powder
and salt.

· · ·

1-1½	pounds fish fillets (orange roughy, flounder, snapper or other white fish)
1	tablespoon Dijon-style mustard
1	tablespoon honey
2	teaspoons freshly squeezed lemon juice
½	teaspoon curry powder
	Salt and freshly ground pepper to taste

Preheat the oven to 450 degrees.

Place fish in a single layer in an ovenproof baking dish. Mix remaining ingredients in a small bowl and spread over fish.

Bake for 10 to 15 minutes, or until the fish flakes easily (cooking time depends on thickness of fillets).

Serves 4. ∾ Serve with rice and steamed broccoli.

Teriyaki Salmon

· ·

T HE TYPICAL TERIYAKI SAUCE contains sherry, but you can make this recipe even if you don't have any. Garlic, ginger and orange zest give a delicious flavoring to the fish, which can either be prepared in advance and marinated or grilled or broiled immediately.

½   cup soy sauce
¼   cup vegetable oil
¼   cup dry sherry (optional)
2   garlic cloves, finely chopped
2   tablespoons grated fresh ginger
1   tablespoon grated tangerine or orange zest
    (orange part of rind only)
2   pounds salmon steaks or fillets

If you are not planning to marinate salmon in advance, preheat the grill or broiler, with a rack about 4 inches from the heat source.

Combine soy sauce, oil, sherry (if using), garlic, ginger and zest in a nonmetallic casserole dish. Add salmon steaks or fillets, turning to coat all sides with marinade. (The salmon can be prepared in advance, covered, and marinated in the refrigerator for up to 24 hours. But it will also taste good without being marinated.)

Grill or broil salmon until it has achieved desired doneness, about 10 minutes for each inch of thickness.

Serves 6 to 8.   ∾   Serve with hot rice and a tossed salad.

Snapper Veracruz

· · · · · · · · · · · · · · · · · ·

ONE OF MY FIRST EXPERIMENTS with fish was this recipe, and it has remained a favorite for years. The dish is a simple one—basically a tomato sauce seasoned with oregano and olives. The smaller you chop the tomatoes before they go into the skillet, the faster the dish will cook. When it's the texture you like, add the fish and 10 minutes later, you're ready for dinner.

2	tablespoons olive oil or vegetable oil
1	medium onion, chopped
1	small garlic clove, minced
1	16-ounce can tomatoes
¼-½	cup chopped stuffed green olives, rinsed in cold water
1	teaspoon dried oregano
	Salt and freshly ground pepper
1	pound red snapper or other firm, white fish

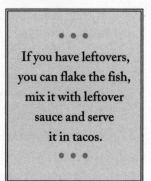

· · ·

If you have leftovers, you can flake the fish, mix it with leftover sauce and serve it in tacos.

· · ·

Heat oil in a large skillet over medium heat. Add onion and garlic and cook for about 5 minutes until softened, stirring occasionally. Drain tomato juice into the skillet.

Chop tomatoes into small pieces and add them to the skillet, along with olives, oregano, salt and pepper. Allow the sauce to simmer until fairly thick. Place fish on top of sauce, cover and simmer for 10 minutes more, or until fish flakes easily with a fork.

Serve fish topped with sauce.

Serves 4. ∾ **Serve with rice and a green vegetable, such as peas.**

Salmon Patties

• • • • • • • • • • • • • • • •

OF ALL THE RECIPES I'VE PRINTED in the newspaper, this one is in the top 20 in terms of reader response. Cooks like the idea of an old-fashioned fish patty that tastes great even though it isn't fried.

¼ cup butter
⅓ cup all-purpose flour
1 cup milk
1 15-ounce can salmon, picked over
   to remove cartilage
2 tablespoons minced onion
1 tablespoon freshly squeezed lemon juice
1 tablespoon minced fresh parsley
1½ cups unseasoned bread crumbs
   Lemon wedges for garnish

• • •
Do not
substitute
seasoned bread
crumbs here.
Use plain.
• • •

Melt butter in a medium saucepan over medium heat. Add flour and stir for 1 minute. Add milk gradually, beating constantly with a wooden spoon or whisk. It will thicken like paste at first; keep beating in more milk to thin it. Bring to a boil; remove from heat. Stir in salmon, onion, lemon juice and parsley. Stir in ½ cup bread crumbs.

Place remaining 1 cup bread crumbs on a large plate. Lightly oil a cookie sheet.

Form salmon mixture into 4 patties and dip both sides into bread crumbs. If you have time, chill patties for at least 30 minutes before placing them on the cookie sheet. Preheat the oven to 400 degrees.

Bake for 25 minutes, or until patties are hot throughout. Garnish with lemon wedges.

Serves 4. ∽ Serve with sweet potatoes and broccoli.

Vegetarian Main Meals

ONCE, WHEN I WAS IN MY relentlessly uncompromising vegetarian stage, I dropped in on an old college friend who panicked at the thought of feeding me. To help her out, I ran to the store and picked up Campbell's tomato soup and saltines. That's meatless cooking at its simplest.

Vegetarian cooking doesn't have to be as pedestrian as canned soup, but neither does it have to be intimidating. Dinners prepared without meat can be as easy—or as complicated—as those with meat.

You can avoid angst in your initial

attempts at meatless cooking if you bear in mind some of the little-known realities about it:

● *Vegetarian food does not always include tofu, or worse, tempeh.* (Tofu is just a little less weird than tempeh.) Some vegetarians like these soybean-derived foods, but neither of them is critical to our already protein-rich diet. Don't think you have to include meat analogs or meat substitutes in each meal in order to be healthy. Like everyone else, vegetarians need to eat loads of fruit, vegetables, grains and beans.

● *Vegetarian cooking doesn't necessarily take long to prepare.* Meatless meals can be as easy and simple as spaghetti sauce over pasta or as time-consuming as acorn squash stuffed with wild rice, fennel and currants. On the nights that I feel desperate about dinner, my favorite dinner is vegetarian—bean burritos

(page 147). They consist of just four ingredients: bottled salsa, green chilies, beans and tortillas. If I can press the children into service, they have grated cheese with them too.

● *Vegetarian food isn't boring.* Don't believe it. Some cooks just can't imagine a dinner plate without meat. When my brother gave up meat in 1972, he went from eating hamburgers and fries to eating cheese pizza and fries. That *was* boring. But there are entire cultures based on vegetarian or nearly vegetarian food. We are lucky enough to be able to choose from all of them: Indian samosas (pastries filled with vegetables), spinach calzones, Vietnamese vegetable rolls.

MANY OF THE meatless main dishes in this chapter can swing both ways: add sausage to a pizza or chicken to black-eyed peas, and you'll satisfy a meat eater.

vegetarian

French Bread Pizza

• • • • • • • • • • • • • • • • • • • •

Put too much cheese and meat on a pizza, and it ends up fat-heavy and calorie-heavy. But if we trim the meat and cheese and make the crust bigger, we increase the amount of complex carbohydrates in the meal, improving its overall nutrition profile. Top the pizza with the leanest meat and lots of vegetables, and a good food becomes even better.

The quickest way to a pizza with more crust than topping is to use French bread.

1	15-inch loaf French bread
1	8-ounce can tomato sauce
1	large garlic clove, chopped
1	teaspoon dried oregano
¾-1	cup grated provolone, Havarti, fontina or other cheese
2-4	tablespoons chopped green bell pepper or stuffed olives

• • •
Since loaf sizes differ from store to store, keep your eye on the pizza as it cooks.
• • •

Preheat the oven to 400 degrees.

Cut bread in half lengthwise, place on a cookie sheet and bake for about 5 minutes to toast the cut side lightly. (You can place it in the preheating oven as you mix sauce and prepare remaining ingredients.)

Combine tomato sauce, garlic and oregano.

Spread a little tomato sauce on cut sides of bread. Distribute some cheese and green pepper or olives over bread; sprinkle with remaining cheese. Bake until cheese has melted, about 15 or 20 minutes.

Serves 2 to 4. ～ **Serve with a tossed salad or with marinated beans and broccoli.**

Basic Italian Tomato Sauce

· ·

AFTER RELYING ON CANNED SPAGHETTI SAUCES for many years, one night I got tired of them—too sweet and bland. They've improved a lot in the last few years, and I always keep some in the house. But I make my own sauce whenever I can. This one was designed to use the plethora of fresh tomatoes in the garden, but it can be made with canned tomatoes too. It takes a little more time than the next recipe.

3	tablespoons olive oil
2	medium onions, chopped
3-4	garlic cloves, minced
3	pounds fresh tomatoes, peeled and chopped, or three 16-ounce cans whole tomatoes
1	6-ounce can tomato paste
¼	cup chopped fresh parsley
1	teaspoon dried oregano
1	teaspoon dried basil
	Salt and freshly ground pepper to taste

· · ·

This recipe
freezes well and
can be multiplied
easily. A larger
quantity of sauce
may require longer
simmering to remove
the excess liquid.

· · ·

Heat oil over high heat in a wide, deep pan, such as a Dutch oven. Add onions and garlic, and cook, stirring, for 5 minutes, or until softened; lower the heat if necessary to prevent burning.

Add tomatoes, squeezing them through your fingers or cutting them into pieces as you add them to the pot. Cook for 5 minutes to reduce liquid. Stir in tomato paste, herbs, salt and pepper, and cook for 5 minutes over high heat, or until sauce has thickened.

Makes about 1 quart. ❧ Use as is on spaghetti or other noodles,
or combine it with hamburger or browned Italian sausage. You can also
use it for pork chops, chicken or chuck roast.

vegetarian

Quick Tomato Sauce

· ·

I MAKE THIS RECIPE when I can handle little more than opening a can. This is almost as easy as store-bought sauce but tastes better.

1 tablespoon olive oil or vegetable oil
1-2 garlic cloves, minced
1 28-ounce can crushed tomatoes,
     packed in puree
2-3 teaspoons Italian herb seasoning or mix
     dried basil, oregano and/or thyme
Salt and freshly ground pepper to taste

· · ·
You can add
1 pound ground
beef, browning it
after cooking
the garlic.
· · ·

Heat oil in a large skillet over medium heat. Add garlic and cook for about 2 minutes, until softened. Add tomatoes, herbs, salt and pepper.

Let sauce simmer, uncovered, while you prepare the rest of the dish (broil eggplant for Eggplant Parmesan, page 138, or cook pasta), for 10 to 15 minutes, or until thickened as desired.

Serves 4 as a topping for spaghetti. ∾ Serve over spaghetti or
broiled eggplant for Eggplant Parmesan.

Eggplant Parmesan

· ·

Eggplant Parmesan can be messy, time-consuming and fattening—but it doesn't have to be.

2	medium eggplants, peeled, if desired
3-4	tablespoons olive oil
	Quick Tomato Sauce (page 137)
½	pound mozzarella cheese, grated
1	cup grated Parmesan cheese

Preheat the broiler, with a rack about 4 inches from the heat source. Brush a cookie sheet lightly with oil.

Slice eggplant into disks about ½ inch thick. Place eggplant slices on the cookie sheet and broil on both sides until they turn light brown and shrink a little, about 5 minutes per side.

Reduce the heat to 400 degrees. Spread a little tomato sauce over the bottom of a 9-by-13-inch baking pan or other large casserole dish. Top with a layer of eggplant. Sprinkle with half of the mozzarella cheese and repeat the layers. Top with Parmesan cheese.

Bake for 25 minutes, until cheeses are melted and dish is bubbly.

Serves 6. ∾ Serve with rotini or spaghetti and a green vegetable.

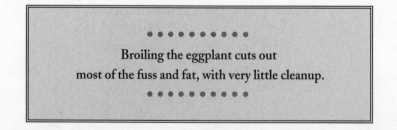

· · · · · · · · · ·
Broiling the eggplant cuts out
most of the fuss and fat, with very little cleanup.
· · · · · · · · · ·

Spaghetti with Red Sauce

· ·

T HIS SAUCE IS CHUNKY AND LIGHT. If you like a thicker, more traditional sauce, add 2 tablespoons of tomato paste and a little water, broth or wine to thin it.

1	tablespoon vegetable oil
1	small onion, sliced
3	garlic cloves, minced
1	28-ounce can crushed tomatoes
1	teaspoon dried basil
	Salt and freshly ground pepper to taste
¼-½	pound linguine or spaghetti

Put a large pot of salted water on to boil.

Heat oil in a large skillet over medium-high heat. Add onion and garlic and cook until they begin to brown, about 10 minutes. Stir in tomatoes, basil, salt and pepper.

Cook, stirring frequently, for about 15 minutes, or until sauce is thick.

Meanwhile, cook noodles in the boiling water until barely tender, about 10 minutes.

Serves 2 generously.

Variation

Red Clam Sauce: Add one or two 6½-ounce cans of drained chopped clams to this sauce.

Spaghetti with Cauliflower

· ·

As a DYED-IN-THE-WOOL BEET HATER, I am reluctant to recommend dishes by saying, "This will convince even the most ardent _____ hater."

But this cauliflower dish is an exception to my rule. I've fed it to cauliflower haters who love it.

3   tablespoons olive oil
3   garlic cloves, crushed
1   medium head cauliflower, broken into
      1-inch florets
     Salt to taste
2   cups spaghetti sauce, store-bought or
      homemade (page 136)
1   pound thin spaghetti
1   cup Cheddar cheese
½   cup grated Parmesan cheese

Put a large pot of salted water on to boil.

Heat 2 tablespoons oil in a deep, heavy skillet with an ovenproof handle over low heat. Add garlic and cook for several minutes, until softened. Add cauliflower and sprinkle with salt. Cook over medium-high heat, stirring occasionally, for about 8 minutes, until cauliflower begins to soften. Add spaghetti sauce, cover and simmer for 10 minutes, or until cauliflower is tender.

Meanwhile, cook spaghetti in the boiling water until cooked through but still firm, about 8 to 10 minutes. Drain and toss with remaining 1 tablespoon oil.

Place spaghetti on individual plates or on a platter and top with cauliflower. Toss and sprinkle with cheeses.

Serves 4 to 6.   ∼   Serve with green peas.

Monterey Rice

. . . .

MANY COOKS ARE FORCED TO EXPLORE VEGETARIANISM by another family member, often a child, who has unilaterally declared that he or she will no longer eat meat. This rice casserole filled a need for several of my friends who were confronted at dinnertime by instant vegetarians. It doesn't require lots of original thinking. The newly declared vegetarian will like it because it contains no meat; the rest of the family will eat it because it tastes good.

4	cups cooked long-grain white rice (from 2 cups raw)
1½	cups shredded Monterey Jack cheese
1	17-ounce can cream-style corn
1	8-ounce can tomato sauce
1	bunch green onions, trimmed and chopped
1	4-ounce can chopped mild green chilies
½	teaspoon salt
¼	teaspoon freshly ground pepper
¼	teaspoon cayenne pepper, or to taste

> • • •
> If your children balk at canned green chilies, substitute sautéed fresh green or red bell peppers.
> • • •

Preheat the oven to 400 degrees.

Combine all ingredients in a medium bowl. Pour into a lightly oiled 1½-quart casserole dish. Bake for 20 minutes if rice is hot, 40 minutes if chilled; cheese should melt.

Serves 4 as a main dish. ～ **Serve with broccoli and rolls.**

Variation

Speedy Tex-Mex Rice: Combine 2 cups cooked rice with 1 cup cottage cheese, one 4-ounce can chopped mild green chilies and 1 teaspoon chili powder. Stir, place in a 1½-quart casserole dish and top with 1 cup grated Cheddar cheese. Bake at 350 degrees until cheese melts, about 15 minutes.

Vegetarian

Pizza-Style Frittata

· ·

UNLIKE AN OMELET, which requires dexterity and split-second timing, a frittata takes absolutely no skill to make. The eggs are simply poured into a hot skillet and briefly baked in a hot oven.

Although the days of eggs and sausage for daily breakfasts may have waned, keep in mind that eggs have a lot going for them. They are high in protein, cheap and make an instant dinner.

12	large eggs
½	cup water
½-1	teaspoon salt
½	teaspoon freshly ground pepper
2-3	tablespoons olive oil or vegetable oil
1	cup diced tomatoes (fresh or canned, drained)
1	cup sliced mushrooms
1	medium onion, sliced
	Pinch of dried oregano and dried basil
¼-⅓	pound shredded mozzarella cheese

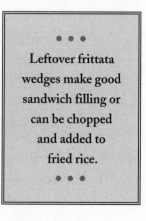

· · ·

Leftover frittata wedges make good sandwich filling or can be chopped and added to fried rice.

· · ·

Preheat the oven to 450 degrees. Place an ovenproof 10- or 12-inch skillet in the oven.

In a large bowl, whisk eggs together with water, salt and pepper.

Remove the skillet from the oven and add 2 tablespoons oil. Add tomatoes, mushrooms, onion, oregano and basil to the skillet, and cook over medium-high heat, adding remaining 1 tablespoon oil, if necessary, until onions have softened, about 15 minutes.

Reduce heat to medium. Pour egg mixture into the skillet and cook until it is partially set. Top with shredded cheese. Place in the oven until cheese melts, about 4 minutes.

Cut into wedges and serve immediately.

Serves 4. ∾ Serve with hot rolls.

vegetarian

Bulgur Salad

• • • • • • • • • •

BULGUR IS MADE FROM GRAINS OF WHOLE WHEAT that have been cracked, cooked and dried. Like Minute Rice, bulgur reconstitutes rapidly and makes a great choice for fast dinners. It can be found in the "health food" department of many supermarkets or with the beans and rice.

If you don't have bulgur, substitute couscous, noodles or cooked rice. The grains and beans in this dish make a high-protein, high-carbohydrate meal that's good in summer. Omit the currants only if you must—they are a whimsical counterpoint to the otherwise practical ingredients.

1½   cups water
1½   cups bulgur
¼   cup wine vinegar
3   tablespoons soy sauce
1   tablespoon olive oil
1   garlic clove, minced
2   carrots, peeled and grated
1   bunch green onions, trimmed and finely
     chopped (about ½ cup)
1   cup dried currants
1   16-ounce can garbanzo beans (chickpeas)

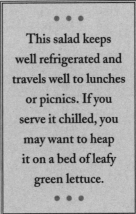

• • •

This salad keeps well refrigerated and travels well to lunches or picnics. If you serve it chilled, you may want to heap it on a bed of leafy green lettuce.

• • •

Bring water to a boil in a medium saucepan. Add bulgur, turn off heat, cover and set aside for 30 minutes.

Meanwhile, beat vinegar, soy sauce, olive oil and garlic together in a medium-size bowl. Stir in carrots, green onions, currants and undrained beans. Add plumped bulgur and stir to blend well.

Serve warm, at room temperature or cold.

Serves 4 as a main dish, 6 as a side dish. ◦ **Serve with fruit salad and bread.**

Black-Eyed Peas and Noodles

THIS RECIPE MEETS ALL MY REQUIREMENTS: it's easy to prepare, tastes great and is good for you. Best of all, my children love it. I make tons of it at a time and freeze the extra. I usually serve it over noodles, but I've also thinned it with water or chicken broth to make soup.

3	tablespoons olive oil
2	medium onions, chopped
2	carrots, trimmed and finely chopped
3-4	garlic cloves, minced
2	16-ounce cans black-eyed peas
1	cup chicken broth (from one 14-ounce can)
	or water
2	teaspoons dried oregano
½	teaspoon crushed red pepper (optional)
1	teaspoon salt, or to taste
½	teaspoon freshly ground pepper
¾	pound spaghetti or vermicelli
	Grated Parmesan cheese (optional)
	Chopped red bell pepper (optional)

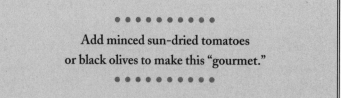

Add minced sun-dried tomatoes
or black olives to make this "gourmet."

Put a large pot of salted water on to boil.

Heat oil in a large skillet over medium heat. Add onions, carrots and garlic, and sauté until they are softened, about 15 minutes, stirring often so they don't brown; they will reduce in size.

Add black-eyed peas, chicken broth or water, oregano, red pepper (if using), salt and pepper, and simmer until thickened, about 5 to 10 minutes.

Meanwhile, cook spaghetti or vermicelli in the boiling water until cooked through but slightly firm, about 8 to 10 minutes.

Drain pasta and serve, topped with black-eyed peas and sprinkled with Parmesan cheese or chopped red bell pepper, if desired.

Serves 4. ∾ **Serve with sautéed green cabbage or spinach, or with a green salad.**

El Paso Pilaf

· · · · · · · · · · · · · · ·

CANNED BEANS ARE THE PERFECT HEALTH FOOD for rushed cooks. They are easy on the budget and, unlike many other foods labeled "healthy," need little more than a brief heating. Canned black-eyed peas, spicy chili beans, black beans, pintos, white beans—all have a place on my cabinet shelves. In the following dish, I use red beans, but you can substitute any beans you like.

· · ·

This dish is also good topped with grated sharp Cheddar.

· · ·

2	teaspoons olive oil
½	medium onion, chopped
1	cup raw long-grain white rice
1¼	cups water or chicken broth (from 1 can)
¼	cup lentils
¼	cup chopped red pepper or canned pimiento
1	14-to-16-ounce can red kidney beans
1	cup corn kernels, fresh, frozen or canned
1	cup chunky bottled salsa
1	teaspoon chili powder, or to taste
1	teaspoon salt
12	slices ripe tomatoes
	Tortilla chips for accompaniment

In a heavy 3-quart pot, heat oil over high heat. Add onions and cook, stirring, for 1 minute. Add rice, water or broth, lentils, red pepper or pimiento, kidney beans, corn, salsa, chili powder and salt; stir to mix.

Bring to a boil, cover, reduce heat and cook for 20 minutes, or until rice and lentils are tender. Stir and serve over tomato slices.

Serves 4 to 6. ∽ Serve with tortilla chips.

Black Bean Burritos

. . . .

WHEN I'M TOO BUSY TO COOK, I make black bean burritos: just a few ingredients, little effort, delicious result, cheaper than delivered pizza. I usually make them from beans that I've cooked in the slow-cooker, then frozen. I pull the beans out of the freezer before I leave for work. If I forget, I thaw them in the microwave when I come home. Canned beans work as well.

10	8-inch whole wheat tortillas or white-flour tortillas
2	16-ounce cans black beans or pinto beans
1	4-ounce can chopped mild green chilies
	Salt and freshly ground pepper to taste
1½-2	cups grated Cheddar cheese, or more to taste
	Approximately 1 cup bottled chunky salsa

Heat tortillas on both sides (for directions, see page 97).

Using a mixer, food processor or a handheld potato masher, mash beans, green chilies, salt and pepper together to desired consistency.

Preheat the oven to 350 degrees. Spread ½ cup salsa in the bottom of a 9-by-13-inch baking dish. Spread about 2 tablespoons bean mixture across 1 tortilla in a long stripe. Sprinkle with a little grated cheese and season with about 1 teaspoon salsa.

Roll up tortilla to enclose filling (leaving ends open) and place in the baking dish, seam side down. Repeat with remaining tortillas.

Sprinkle with remaining cheese and bake for 20 minutes, or until tortillas are heated through.

Serves 4 to 5. ∽ **Serve with apple salad (page 42) and steamed broccoli.**

Hungarian Cabbage
and Noodles

• • • • • • • • • • • • •

PRECHOPPED GARLIC, purchased in little jars in the supermarket produce section, has its limitations. Garlic connoisseurs will roll their eyes when you admit you use it.

So I don't mention it. But I use it all the time. I recommend it to speed things along in the following dish, which is so rich in anticarcinogenic cabbage and high-carbohydrate noodles that the Surgeon General could serve it with pride.

1	medium head green cabbage, chopped
2	tablespoons water
1	medium onion, finely chopped
1	teaspoon minced garlic clove
1	tablespoon light brown sugar
1	teaspoon Worcestershire sauce
1	teaspoon dried thyme
½	teaspoon paprika
	Salt and freshly ground pepper to taste
½	pound bow tie noodles or other broad, flat noodles
1-2	tablespoons butter

Put a large pot of salted water on to boil.

Place cabbage in a large skillet with a tight-fitting lid. Add water, onion, garlic, sugar and seasonings. Cover and steam for 20 to 30 minutes, until very tender, stirring occasionally. Watch carefully so it doesn't burn, adding a small amount of water, if necessary.

Cook noodles in the boiling water for about 12 to 15 minutes, or until cooked through but still slightly firm.

Drain noodles well and add to skillet with cabbage, along with butter. Stir to combine.

Serves 4. ∽ **Serve with fried apples and rolls.**

Vegetarian Chili

· · · · · · · · · · · · · · · · · ·

THIS CHILI CONTAINS an abundance of complex carbohydrates and fresh vegetables. It's my daughter's favorite dish, and has been since she was three.

Strictly speaking, unless you already have the common herbs and spices called for here, you won't be able to get through the express lane, but it's so easy to make a large quantity of this chili that I've included it anyway.

1	cup tomato juice
1	cup bulgur
3	tablespoons olive oil or vegetable oil
2	medium onions, chopped
2	medium carrots, chopped small
1	green bell pepper, seeded, cored and chopped small
2	garlic cloves, minced
¼	cup chili powder
2	teaspoons ground cumin
1	teaspoon dried oregano
½	teaspoon cayenne pepper, or to taste
1	4-ounce can chopped mild green chilies
1	28-ounce can tomatoes
6	cups cooked or canned kidney beans (three 16-ounce cans)
	Salt and freshly ground pepper to taste
	Grated Cheddar, Muenster or Monterey Jack cheese (optional)

vegetarian

Bring tomato juice to a boil in a small saucepan and add bulgur; set aside, covered, off the heat.

Heat oil over medium heat in a large, wide pot or Dutch oven. Add onions and cook, stirring occasionally until softened, for 5 to 10 minutes. Add carrots, green pepper and garlic and cook until carrots are barely tender, about 10 minutes more. Add spices and stir for about 1 minute; stir in green chilies.

Add canned tomatoes with their juice, chopping coarsely or squeezing them through your fingers as you add them to the pot. Stir in kidney beans and bulgur-tomato juice mixture; stir to mix well.

Bring to a boil, reduce heat to low and cook for 20 minutes (or longer, if desired) to blend the flavors, stirring occasionally. If necessary, thin to desired consistency with water or tomato juice; add salt and pepper.

Serve hot, topped with grated cheese, if desired.

Serves 8. ➴ **Serve with carrots and celery sticks.**

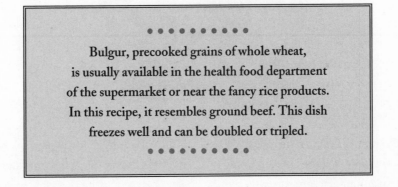

• • • • • • • • • •

Bulgur, precooked grains of whole wheat,
is usually available in the health food department
of the supermarket or near the fancy rice products.
In this recipe, it resembles ground beef. This dish
freezes well and can be doubled or tripled.

• • • • • • • • • •

Vegetables & Side Dishes

VEGETABLES ARE OFTEN the first casualty of rushed meal-planning. I'm not sure why, but cooks in a hurry will give some thought to meat, make an effort with the starchy side dish but give little or no consideration to the vegetables, balking at anything more elaborate than frozen or canned.

Surveys show that people think eating healthfully takes too much time and the bottleneck is usually the vegetable preparation—and they are not entirely mistaken.

Washing spinach is tedious. Cutting a butternut squash in two can require a bigger and sharper knife than many people own. Peas take shelling, cauliflower requires breaking, corn needs shucking.

Frozen vegetables, on the other hand, lack panache. They have the advantage of convenience, but looking at them on the plate, nobody is likely to say, "Hey! Wow! Frozen vegetables for ME?"

T HOSE OF US IN PURSUIT of good health, a colorful plate, varied textures and different flavors need to find easy ways to serve vegetables and fruits. Here are a few suggestions that work for me and other experienced family cooks I know:

• Serve fresh apple slices, carrot sticks or banana with pizza.

• Have salad as often as possible, even if you're serving a vegetable. Lettuce can be washed two or three days in advance; cold, cooked and marinated vegetables can be served as salad.

• Use pasta and rice salads as vehicles for extra vegetables. For example, you can blanch broccoli and peas, and add them to cooked rotini, along with some crumbled feta cheese, some chopped olives and an oil-and-vinegar dressing. Season with oregano or Dijon mustard, salt and pepper.

• Plan one vegetarian meal each week. That can be a vegetable plate with sweet potato rounds, rice, cooked kale and raw carrots; or a more elaborate dish like stir-fried vegetables over rice; pasta with a sauce of stewed tomatoes; or vegetable soup.

• Have on hand a prepared dressing or sauce that you can toss with plain vegetables. Leftover carrots, broccoli and cauliflower are delicious dressed and served cold.

• Put cooked peas in rice or pasta side dishes. They are pretty and nutritious. So is diced red bell pepper.

In my family, very few vegetables show up in a pile on the plate. We're more likely to pass a platter of raw cut-up cauliflower, carrots and celery to be eaten with a low-fat dip. Or I make soup with turkey broth that hides bits of turnip among the more acceptable carrots, tomatoes and green pepper. My bean soup comes studded with greens; my vegetarian chili has green peppers, carrots, onions and tomatoes.

When you need a simple vegetable and want something more elaborate than frozen green beans, try a few of these quick ideas.

Sautéed Asparagus

· ·

ORIENTAL SESAME OIL is deep brown and smells of toasted nuts. A little bit goes a long way, so you get maximum flavor for minimum calories. Don't confuse this sesame oil with a milder type that's golden and usually sold near the other vegetable oils. Oriental sesame oil is found in most supermarkets near the other Asian foods. If can't find it there, you can find it in Asian markets.

- 2 tablespoons vegetable oil
- 2 pounds asparagus, trimmed and cut into 2-inch pieces
- ½ cup water or chicken broth
- ½ teaspoon sugar
  Salt to taste
- 1 tablespoon soy sauce
- 1 teaspoon toasted sesame oil

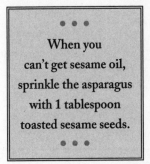

· · ·

When you can't get sesame oil, sprinkle the asparagus with 1 tablespoon toasted sesame seeds.

· · ·

Heat oil over high heat in a large skillet or wok. When oil is hot, add asparagus. Stir several times, reduce heat to medium-high and add water or broth, sugar and salt. Cover and cook for about 4 minutes, stirring once or twice; asparagus should be bright green and crunchy.

Uncover, increase the heat to high and cook to evaporate liquid, about 1 minute. Remove to a serving bowl or a plate and drizzle with soy sauce and sesame oil.

Serves 4 to 6.

Green Beans with Almonds

· ·

ADDING TOASTED NUTS, seeds or even a little meat makes vegetables a whole lot more interesting than if they were steamed and served plain.

2-3	cups trimmed green beans (about ¾ pound)
½	cup water
1	tablespoon vegetable oil
2-3	tablespoons almonds or sunflower seeds, chopped
	Salt and freshly ground pepper to taste

· · ·

If you have
fresh herbs, add a
little fresh oregano,
mint or thyme.

· · ·

Bring water to a boil in a wide skillet. Add green beans, cover and cook 10 minutes, or until barely tender, shaking the skillet occasionally to redistribute beans. Drain, leaving beans in the colander.

Add oil to the skillet and add almonds or sunflower seeds. Stir over medium heat until almonds or seeds turn light brown.

Return beans to the skillet, tossing with nuts. Season with salt and pepper and reheat thoroughly.

Serves 4.

Sesame Green Beans

• •

Broccoli is equally delicious prepared this way.

1   tablespoon olive oil
1   tablespoon sesame seeds
1   pound green beans, trimmed and
      cut into 2-inch lengths
¼   cup chicken broth or water
¼   teaspoon salt
    Freshly ground pepper to taste

> • • •
> Chop leftovers
> fine and stuff into
> pita bread with
> chicken or cheese.
> • • •

Heat oil in a large skillet over medium heat. Add sesame seeds, and when they start to darken, add green beans. Cook, stirring, until beans turn bright green. Add broth or water, salt and pepper.

Cover and cook on medium heat until beans are as tender as you like, about 10 minutes (if you cook them longer, you may need to add more liquid), or until they are bright green and firm but slightly tender.

Uncover and boil away excess liquid. Taste and adjust seasonings.

Serves 4.

Broccoli with Raisins

• •

IT MAY SOUND LIKE AN UNLIKELY COMBINATION, but the concentrated sweetness of raisins complements broccoli.

1   large head broccoli (about 1½ pounds),
     trimmed, stems peeled
2   teaspoons freshly squeezed lemon juice
1   shallot, sliced, or 2 green onions, finely
     chopped
2   tablespoons raisins
½   cup toasted walnuts or pine nuts
¼   cup olive oil
1   tablespoon good-quality vinegar
     (wine vinegar or balsamic vinegar)
2   tablespoons grated Parmesan cheese

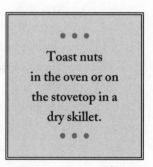

• • •

Toast nuts
in the oven or on
the stovetop in a
dry skillet.

• • •

Preheat the oven to 250 degrees, if you plan to serve broccoli hot.

Bring a large pot of water to a boil; add broccoli. Cook until bright green and barely tender, about 5 minutes. Drain and rinse in cold water. Cut into bite-size pieces and place in an ovenproof serving dish. Sprinkle with lemon juice. Add shallot or green onions to broccoli, along with raisins, nuts, oil, vinegar and Parmesan.

Rewarm broccoli in the oven, if desired. Serve warm or at room temperature.

Serves 4 to 6.

vegetables & side dishes

Savory Broccoli

• • • • • • • • • • • • • • • • • • •

THIS DISH IS PRETTIEST when it's made with broccoli florets. At my house, serving florets is one way to guarantee that I don't end up with piles of cut-up stems on the plates after dinner. On the other hand, if you can't picture yourself setting aside the stems "for another use," feel free to chop them and add them to this dish (peel them first). The seasoned olive oil does wonders for broccoli.

1	large head broccoli (about 1½ pounds), washed; florets and stems separated
2	tablespoons olive oil
1	onion, chopped
4	garlic cloves, minced
1	teaspoon dried oregano
1	teaspoon salt
½	teaspoon ground cumin
2-4	tablespoons water

> • • •
> Broccoli stems
> can be peeled and cut
> into thin, lengthwise
> pieces for salads
> or stir-fries.
> • • •

Cut broccoli florets into bite-size pieces. (Set aside stems for another use.) Heat oil over medium-high heat, add onion and sauté until transparent, 5 to 10 minutes. Add garlic to the skillet and stir over medium heat until softened, about 2 minutes.

Add oregano, salt, cumin and broccoli pieces and stir constantly for about 2 minutes. Add water, cover, and simmer for 10 minutes, or until broccoli is bright green and tender.

Serves 4.

Lemon Broccoli

• • • • • • • • • • • • • • • •

STEAMING VEGETABLES IN A WIDE SKILLET cooks them more evenly than in a deep pot because the steam doesn't have to penetrate several layers. Put 2 inches of water in a wide skillet and place a collapsible steamer (it looks like a flower with metal petals punched full of holes) in it. Put the prepared vegetables on top, cover and bring water to a boil. Steam the vegetables until they are tender.

1   large head broccoli (about 1½ pounds),
       separated into florets and stems
1   tablespoon melted butter or olive oil
     Juice of 1 lemon
     Salt and freshly ground pepper to taste

Peel broccoli stems, if using. Place broccoli in a vegetable steamer or in a small amount of water in a large skillet. Cover and steam or boil over high heat until tender, about 10 to 15 minutes.

Mix butter or oil with lemon juice, salt and pepper in a small dish. Place broccoli in a serving dish and drizzle with butter mixture. Toss to coat, and serve.

Serves 4.

Italian-Style Cabbage

· ·

Freshly grated Parmesan cheese and good-quality ham make this sensational. Because it's special and savory, this cabbage dish makes a great component on a "vegetable plate."

1	tablespoon olive oil
½	medium onion, chopped
½	teaspoon fennel seeds (optional)
¼	cup thinly sliced flavorful ham, such as country ham or Smithfield ham
4	cups chopped cabbage (from ½ medium head)
	Salt and freshly ground pepper to taste
2-4	tablespoons grated Parmesan cheese

Heat oil over medium-high heat in a large skillet. Add onion, fennel seeds (if using) and ham and cook until onion is translucent, about 10 minutes, stirring frequently.

Add cabbage, cover and cook for 5 minutes. Uncover and continue cooking until all liquid is evaporated and cabbage is tender, about 15 minutes or even longer, if you like it very tender. Stir in salt and pepper. Sprinkle with Parmesan cheese, and serve.

Serves 4. ∽ **Serve with pan-fried chicken breast, pork chops or cube steak.**

Ginger-Lemon Carrots

CARROTS AT MY HOUSE are usually served raw, cut into sticks. But some nights I get a little fancier, if the main dish is plain, or if I've volunteered to contribute the vegetable to a group effort. That's where this recipe comes in handy.

1   pound carrots, trimmed; peeled, if desired
1   tablespoon butter
1   tablespoon sugar or honey
1   tablespoon freshly squeezed lemon juice
1   teaspoon grated lemon zest
     (yellow part of rind only)
1   teaspoon grated fresh ginger or ¼ teaspoon
     ground ginger

Slice carrots into 3-inch sticks about ½ inch thick. Melt butter in a large skillet. Add carrots, cover and cook over medium-high heat, shaking the pan occasionally, until carrots are barely cooked, about 5 to 10 minutes. The high heat may brown some carrots, but that's all right.

Add sugar or honey, lemon juice, lemon zest and ginger; stir well. Cover, reduce heat to low and cook, stirring occasionally, until sugar is dissolved and carrots are done, about 5 to 10 minutes.

Serves 6.

vegetables & side dishes

Oven-Roasted Carrots

· ·

OVEN-ROASTING DOES WONDERFUL THINGS for nearly every vegetable. But since carrots are cheap, plentiful and a constant resident of our vegetable bin, they are what I roast most often.

Not a bad choice, considering that dark orange vegetables are full of beta-carotene, a powerful cancer fighter.

3	tablespoons olive oil
1	pound carrots, peeled and cut into sticks 3 inches long by ½ inch wide
3-5	large garlic cloves
1	tablespoon vinegar (any kind) Salt and freshly ground pepper, to taste

Preheat the oven to 425 degrees.

Spread 2 tablespoons oil on a cookie sheet. Scatter carrots across the pan. Cut each garlic clove into 2 or 3 pieces and scatter among carrots. Drizzle with remaining 1 tablespoon oil and vinegar. Bake for 15 minutes, stirring occasionally; carrots should brown but not burn—they will not be brown all over. Remove from the oven and season with salt and pepper.

Serve hot, cold or at room temperature.

Serves 4 to 6.

· · · · · · · · · ·

Leftover carrots can be added to tossed salad
or served cold as part of a vegetable platter. Green beans
or cauliflower may be substituted in this recipe.

· · · · · · · · · ·

163

Express Lane Cookbook

Marinated Cauliflower

· ·

THIS CAULIFLOWER IS MORE PICKLED than marinated, like those pickled mushrooms you'll sometimes find on a cold plate or at cocktail parties.

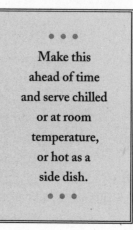

· · ·

Make this ahead of time and serve chilled or at room temperature, or hot as a side dish.

· · ·

2   cups cauliflower florets (about ½ of a large head)
1   teaspoon dried oregano
¾   cup wine vinegar or apple cider vinegar
¼   cup water
1   garlic clove, crushed
1   teaspoon mustard seeds
1   whole clove
1   teaspoon salt
½   teaspoon freshly ground pepper
3   tablespoons olive oil

Cook cauliflower in a large pot of boiling water until barely tender, about 4 to 5 minutes. Place cooked cauliflower in a nonaluminum bowl and toss with oregano.

In a small saucepan, bring vinegar, water, garlic, mustard seeds, clove, salt and pepper to a boil. Pour over cauliflower and stir in oil. Serve hot, warm or cold.

Serves 6 to 8. ∾ **Serve with hamburgers or grilled chicken, or chop it fine and add to a chilled pasta salad.**

Variation

Marinated Vegetables and Olives: Stuffed green or imported black olives are a delicious addition. Add about ½ cup olives to the vegetables. Pit black olives first.

Oven-Browned French Fries

• •

Y OU CAN SAVE MONEY and calories by making French fries at home, baking rather than frying them.

If making French fries is too inconvenient, you'll be glad to know that some store-bought fries get 30 percent or less of their calories from fat. Among them are these Ore-Ida products: Lite Crinkle Cuts, Home Style Wedges, Dinner Fries, Golden Crinkles and Golden Fries. Other low-fat frozen fries include three McCain products: Classic Cut, Golden Steak Fries and Crinkle Cut. All need to be baked rather than fried in order to get their crispness without added grease.

2   large potatoes, preferably russets,
        peeled, if desired
1-2   tablespoons vegetable oil
        Salt and freshly ground pepper

Preheat the oven to 400 degrees.

Slice potatoes into French-fry shapes, about 3 inches long and ½ inch wide. Spread 1 tablespoon of oil on a wide, shallow roasting pan. Spread potatoes on the pan; sprinkle with salt and pepper. Drizzle with a little more oil.

Bake, stirring occasionally, until potatoes are brown and cooked through, about 20 minutes.

Serves 2 to 4.

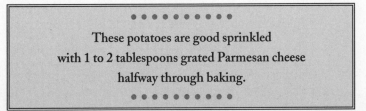

• • • • • • • • • •
These potatoes are good sprinkled
with 1 to 2 tablespoons grated Parmesan cheese
halfway through baking.
• • • • • • • • • •

Potatoes Vinaigrette

· ·

POTATO SALAD DOESN'T REQUIRE the addition of mayonnaise, and potato salad doesn't always have to be cold. This potato salad is tossed with salad dressing and chopped celery.

1	pound small red-skinned or new potatoes, with skins, left whole
1	tablespoon Dijon-style or Pommery mustard
1	tablespoon red wine vinegar
⅓	cup olive oil or vegetable oil
1	celery rib, minced
½	medium onion, minced
½	teaspoon dried rosemary, minced
	Salt and freshly ground pepper to taste

· · ·

Serve this
warm the
night you fix it
and cold the
next day.

· · ·

In a large pot of boiling, salted water, boil potatoes until tender, about 20 minutes. Drain and set aside; cut them into bite-size chunks, if they are large.

In a medium bowl, beat mustard and vinegar together. Using a whisk or fork, beat in oil until smooth. Add celery, onion and rosemary.

Add potatoes; toss to coat with dressing. Season with salt and pepper.

Serves 4. ◞ Serve with hamburgers and cooked or raw carrots.

New Potatoes with Cumin

. . . .

CUMIN AND TURMERIC give these potatoes a definite curried flavor. The dish needs every grain of the salt to taste best.

2	pounds small new potatoes
3-4	tablespoons olive oil
1	teaspoon ground cumin
¼	teaspoon ground turmeric
1	teaspoon salt
	Freshly ground pepper to taste
¼	teaspoon cayenne pepper (optional)

In a large pot of boiling, salted water, boil potatoes until just done, about 20 minutes. Drain and set aside.

Heat oil in a large skillet over medium-high heat. Add cumin and turmeric, stir and add potatoes, salt, pepper and cayenne, if using, stirring to coat potatoes.

Serves 4 generously. ∾ **Serve with "fried" catfish (page 126).**

Sautéed Potatoes

· · · · · · · · · · · · · · · · · · · ·

GRATING POTATOES HELPS them cook quickly. These potatoes taste like the best-ever hash browns. Keep an eye on them, flipping and adjusting the heat if anything seems in danger of burning. High heat crisps the potatoes, but there's a world of difference between dark brown and black.

2 tablespoons vegetable oil or olive oil
1 medium onion, chopped
4 medium potatoes, peeled, if desired
Salt and freshly ground pepper to taste

Heat oil over medium heat in a large skillet. Add onions and cook until just beginning to brown, about 5 to 10 minutes.

Meanwhile, grate potatoes coarsely (or chop them into small cubes).

Add potatoes to the skillet, increase the heat to medium-high and cook for about 15 or 20 minutes, using a spatula to flip them in large sections occasionally and scraping the bottom of the skillet; some potatoes should be crusty, some soft. Cook a little longer, if necessary, adjusting the heat if potatoes seem to be getting too brown. Season with salt and pepper and serve immediately.

Serves 4.

Jacques Pépin's Honey-Baked Sweet Potatoes

. . . .

I WAS BORN AND RAISED in the South, but if anybody ever mentioned sweet potatoes to me, all I pictured was miniature marshmallows and crushed pineapple. It took a Frenchman to make me see my folly. I watched Jacques Pépin make these potatoes. The double-cooking method—first a boil, then a quick fry—helps develop the potatoes' natural sweetness, which gets a boost from a little honey. The preparation goes quickly, but if this dish seems too much work for the average night, try it on Thanksgiving. Salt and pepper are essential to the flavor profile.

3-4	medium sweet potatoes, unpeeled
1	tablespoon vegetable oil or olive oil
	Salt and freshly ground pepper
2	tablespoons butter
2	tablespoons honey

Put a large pot of water on to boil. Slice sweet potatoes into disks about 1½ inches thick. Place them in the boiling water and boil until just tender, about 15 minutes; drain.

Lightly coat a large skillet with oil and heat. Add potatoes, season with salt and a generous amount of pepper, and fry on both sides until speckly brown and tender all the way through, about 10 to 15 minutes.

Combine butter and honey and heat in a saucepan until they are warm, syrupy and well mixed, or combine in a small bowl and microwave for 1 minute on medium power, or until butter melts.

Transfer potatoes to a serving platter with a spatula and drizzle with honey-butter mixture.

Serves 6.

Oven-Roasted Vegetable Medley

• • • • • •

MY FAVORITE VEGETABLES are those that have been roasted, preferably with a generous amount of whole garlic cloves and onion quarters. Make this dish with any combination of vegetables you prefer, using the following recipe as guidance. Leftovers can be sprinkled with a teaspoon or two of vinegar and eaten cold, like a salad.

1	medium onion, quartered
1	large potato, peeled, if desired
1	large carrot, washed and trimmed
1	leek, white part only (optional)
1	small eggplant, peeled, if desired
2	tablespoons olive oil, or to taste
½	teaspoon salt, or to taste
½	teaspoon freshly ground pepper
2	garlic cloves, left whole

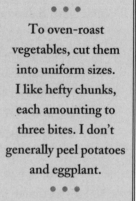

• • •

To oven-roast vegetables, cut them into uniform sizes. I like hefty chunks, each amounting to three bites. I don't generally peel potatoes and eggplant.

• • •

Preheat the oven to 400 degrees. Lightly oil a large, shallow roasting pan or a cookie sheet.

Place onion on the pan. Quarter potato, or cut into sixths. Cut carrot in half lengthwise and then, if necessary, cut the thicker end in half again. Cut leek, if using, in half and wash well under running water to remove grit. Cut into 3-inch lengths. Cut eggplant into large chunks.

Place potato, carrot, leek and eggplant in a large bowl with oil, salt and pepper; toss and transfer to the pan. Bake for 10 minutes, add garlic and cook for 10 to 15 minutes more, tossing occasionally, or until vegetables begin to soften and turn brown on the edges.

Serves 2. ∾ Serve with lentils *(recipe follows)* and whole-grain rolls (page 187).

Easy Lentils

. . . .

I LOVE LENTILS because they cook in a fraction of the time of other dried beans. I like to use them to round out a platter of grilled or baked vegetables.

1 cup lentils

3 cups canned tomato juice or one 16-ounce
     can chopped tomatoes, with juice,
     plus 1 cup water

1 teaspoon dried thyme, oregano or basil

1 teaspoon salt

½ teaspoon freshly ground pepper

½ cup crumbled feta or blue cheese
     (about 2-3 ounces)

In a medium saucepan, combine lentils with tomato juice or tomatoes and liquid, herbs, salt and pepper. Bring to a boil, reduce heat, cover and simmer for 40 minutes, or until lentils are soft. Add more water if necessary, but lentils should be fairly dry and separate.

Sprinkle with cheese and serve.

Serves 2 to 4.

Zucchini and Yellow Squash Mélange

•••••••

Mélange is French for "whatever is threatening to take over your garden and needs to be cooked, quick!"

Seriously, this dish could just as easily be made with all zucchini or with just yellow squash or without the onion but with a little garlic. Cook it as long as you like. I've given the politically correct time of 5 minutes below, but I must admit that I like squash cooked for 15 or even 30 minutes. Not as quick as the 5-minute approach, but tasty. Don't be shy with the pepper.

2 tablespoons butter
2 8-inch zucchini
2 8-inch yellow squash
1 red bell pepper, cored and cut into strips
½ red onion, cut lengthwise and sliced thin
½ teaspoon dried basil
Salt and freshly ground pepper

•••
Toss leftovers with pasta or use in fried rice (page 82).
•••

Melt butter in a large skillet. Add vegetables, sprinkle with basil, cover and cook for 5 minutes over medium heat, or until vegetables are done to desired taste.

Season with salt and pepper and serve.

Serves 4.

Green Rice

• • • • • • • • • • •

THERE ARE TIMES WHEN serving plain rice just won't do. Adding leafy greens is one approach.

2 cups chicken broth (one 16-ounce can)
1 cup raw long-grain white rice
1 tablespoon butter
½ teaspoon salt
3 cups finely chopped collard greens or
   mustard greens
Freshly ground pepper and Tabasco
   sauce to taste
Grated Parmesan or crumbled feta cheese
(optional)

• • •

You can
add frozen peas
instead of
greens.

• • •

Bring broth to a boil in a medium saucepan; add rice, butter and salt. Stir, and add greens, a handful at a time, stirring after each addition.

Cover, bring to a boil, reduce heat to a simmer and cook until rice is tender, about 20 minutes. Season with pepper and Tabasco. Sprinkle with a little cheese, if using, before serving.

Serves 4.

Pecan Rice

· · · · · · · · · · · ·

Toasted PECANS ADD an elegant crunch to plain rice. Serve it with expensive but unadorned meats, such as lamb chops or beef or pork tenderloin.

> 1 cup chopped pecans
> 3 tablespoons butter
> 3 cups water
> 1½ cups raw long-grain white rice
> 1 teaspoon salt
> Freshly ground pepper to taste

Combine pecans and butter in a large skillet over medium heat. Toast pecans to a light brown, stirring often; set aside.

Meanwhile, bring water to a boil in a medium saucepan. Add rice and salt; bring to a boil. Stir, reduce heat to low, cover and simmer for 20 minutes, or until rice is tender.

Fluff with a fork and stir in pecan butter and pepper.

Serves 6.

Garlic Rotini

· · · · · · · · · · · · · ·

WHEN YOU WANT TO SERVE more than boiled noodles as a side dish to chicken or beef, try this dish.

½ pound rotini (corkscrew noodles)
3 tablespoons olive oil
4 garlic cloves, minced
    Salt and freshly ground pepper to taste
2-3 tablespoons grated Parmesan cheese
        (freshly grated, if possible)

In a large pot of boiling, salted water, cook noodles until tender but still firm, about 10 minutes.

In a small pan, heat oil over medium-high heat, add garlic and sauté until it just begins to turn golden; set aside.

Drain noodles completely, shaking off excess water. Return noodles to the pot and drizzle over garlic-oil mixture, tossing to coat. Add salt and pepper. Sprinkle with Parmesan cheese and serve.

Serves 4.

Breads

HOT BREAD IS A SYMBOL of hospitality, as it well should be. Nothing says "home cooking" like hot bread fresh out of the oven. But, you may point out, hot bread became that symbol in the hallowed days when cooks had more time.

Luckily, you can serve hot bread at the table without hours of preparation. First, there are quick breads: those that use baking soda and baking powder, not yeast, to get their height. Biscuits and corn bread are the mainstays of the quick-bread group, and they can contribute much to meals.

At my house, hot biscuits help sell a meal. We may be having something the kids don't like, but served with biscuits, it becomes acceptable. Many times when I invite company over after a work day and wonder on the way home, "What the heck am I going to feed these people?" I fry up corn cakes—griddle cakes made with cornmeal—that are buttered and eaten with the fingers.

QUICK BREADS OFTEN aren't good keepers. You'll need to polish them off in a hurry—which is easy—or reheat any leftovers under the broiler the next day, or freeze them.

Bread enthusiasts may sniff and tell you that no yeast bread is acceptable unless it has had a couple of long rises, but perfectly delicious bread can be made on a weeknight schedule by inexperienced cooks. Yeast, after all, is totally democratic: it will work for anyone. It thrives in warm temperatures, but

is killed by too much heat. Treat it right, and you can have good bread or pizza crust in 30 minutes. Skeptics should try my quick whole wheat rolls (page 187).

But bread doesn't have to be homemade to be appealing. Crunchy pita toasts, which are basically a heat-and-serve food, provide contrast to hot soup. Flour tortillas with melted cheese on top make a filling, warm addition to a mostly salad meal.

In this chapter, I've included enough hot bread recipes to show how easy it is to make a good meal great, even when you don't have much time.

breads

Parmesan Pita Toasts

• •

A CRUNCHY PITA TOAST WITH CHEESE TOPPING makes a soup meal more interesting, without making it more complicated. These toasts are tasty, but not too filling.

3   small pita breads
2   tablespoons butter, softened
½   cup grated Parmesan cheese
      Paprika or cayenne pepper (optional)

Preheat the broiler, with a rack 4 inches from the heat source.

Cut pitas in half horizontally. Spread each pita round with butter and sprinkle with cheese and seasoning, if using. Cut each round into quarters (so they are wedge-shaped) and broil for 20 seconds or less, or until lightly browned. Watch carefully; they burn easily.

Serves 4 to 6.

Quick Biscuits

• • • • • • • • • • • • • • •

MY CHILDREN LEARNED TO LOVE LENTILS because they instantly loved the hot biscuits served alongside them. Eventually, biscuits became the first baked goods they learned to make.

Split these horizontally the next morning and spread with butter, sprinkle with cinnamon sugar and broil for a minute or so.

2   cups all-purpose flour
1   tablespoon baking powder
½   teaspoon salt
6   tablespoons butter or margarine
¾   cup milk or buttermilk

• • •

Leftover biscuits can be stored in a plastic bag.

• • •

Preheat the oven to 450 degrees.

In a large bowl, combine dry ingredients. Cut in butter or margarine, using a fork, 2 knives or a pastry blender. When mixture is the texture of coarse meal, add milk or buttermilk and stir until mixture leaves the sides of the bowl and forms a soft, moist dough.

Turn out dough on a floured surface and knead gently, folding it over a couple of times until it is fairly smooth. With a floured rolling pin, roll out dough ¾ inch thick.

Cut with a 2-inch biscuit cutter or a small juice glass and place rounds close together on an ungreased 9-inch round cake pan. Press any remaining dough scraps together, knead and fold a couple of times to smooth, reroll and cut.

Bake for 12 minutes, or until golden brown.

Makes about 9 to 10 biscuits.

Cheddar Biscuits

• • • • • • • • • • • • • • • • • • •

Iɴ ᴍᴀɴʏ ᴄᴀsᴇs, cheese makes biscuits better.

1¾   cups all-purpose flour
1   tablespoon baking powder
½   teaspoon salt
4   tablespoons (½ stick) chilled butter
     or margarine
⅓   cup shredded sharp Cheddar cheese
¾   cup milk

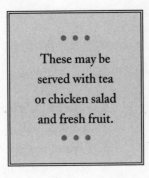

• • •

These may be
served with tea
or chicken salad
and fresh fruit.

• • •

Preheat the oven to 450 degrees.

Combine dry ingredients in a medium-size bowl. Cut in butter or margarine and cheese using a fork, 2 knives or a pastry blender. When mixture is the consistency of coarse meal, add milk and stir just until dough leaves the sides of the bowl.

Turn out dough onto a lightly floured surface and knead gently, folding it over 8 to 10 times so that it is fairly smooth. With a floured rolling poin, roll out dough about ¾ inch thick and cut with a 2-inch biscuit cutter or a small juice glass.

Place rounds close together in an ungreased 9-inch cake pan. Bake for 12 to 15 minutes, until light brown.

Makes about 12 biscuits.

Variation
Substitute Roquefort cheese for Cheddar.

Irish Soda Bread

. . . .

I KNOW A RESTAURANT that includes thin slices of Irish soda bread in the basket of crackers it serves with bowls of homemade soup. The effect is wonderful, and the bread is even easier to make than biscuits.

Irish Soda Bread doesn't require yeast, so it can be ready quickly. Slice it thinly and serve it warm or cold with nearly any meal.

2	cups all-purpose flour
1	teaspoon salt
1	teaspoon sugar
1	teaspoon baking powder
½	teaspoon baking soda
3	tablespoons butter, margarine or shortening
¾	cup buttermilk

• • •

Because soda bread contains little fat, it doesn't store well.

• • •

Preheat the oven to 375 degrees. Butter a cookie sheet.

Combine dry ingredients in a large bowl. Cut in butter, margarine or shortening, using a fork, 2 knives or a pastry blender until mixture is the consistency of coarse meal. Stir in buttermilk. Knead a few times on a lightly floured surface; dough will resemble biscuit dough. Form into a mound about 5 inches in diameter and about 2 inches high.

Place dough on the cookie sheet and slash a cross in the top and down the sides, about 1 inch into dough.

Bake for 35 to 40 minutes, or until loaf sounds hollow when rapped with the fingers.

Cut into slices no more than ½ inch thick.

Serves 6.

Sour Cream Corn Bread

• •

HOT CORN BREAD IS DELICIOUS with meals. Health watchers may panic when they see the sour cream in the recipe below. They shouldn't. The recipe calls for no other fat, and when served with a vegetable-bean soup, tomato soup, chili or even a vegetable plate, this corn bread is a delicious and nutritious addition to the meal.

1	cup all-purpose flour
1	cup yellow cornmeal
1	tablespoon baking powder
½	teaspoon salt
1½	cups sour cream
2	large eggs

Preheat the oven to 400 degrees. Butter an 8-inch square baking pan.

Combine dry ingredients in a medium bowl. Beat sour cream and eggs together in a separate bowl and stir into dry ingredients.

Spoon into the baking pan and bake for 20 minutes, until corn bread is brown around the edges.

Serves 6 to 8.

Corn Cakes

• • • • • • • • • • •

CORN CAKES ARE SERVED ALL OVER THE SOUTH as an accompaniment to bean soup, making a perfect protein complement as well as a simple, satisfying dinner. They are rather like corn pancakes and are easy to make and eater-friendly. I like to prepare them when I have invited another family over for dinner at the last minute. They're also a good choice when I'm serving something the kids aren't wild about.

Butter these corn bread pancakes and eat them with your fingers. If you make the corn cakes for dinner and have leftover batter, refrigerate it and make pancakes in the morning. Cook them the same way, but serve with syrup or jam.

2 large eggs
  About 1½ cups milk (or buttermilk,
    if you have it)
¼ cup vegetable oil, plus a little more
    for greasing the pan
1 cup self-rising cornmeal
1 cup self-rising flour
1 tablespoon sugar (optional)

• • • • • • • • • •

If you don't have self-rising flour and cornmeal,
use regular flour, regular cornmeal and add 1 teaspoon baking
powder and 1 teaspoon salt to the recipe.

• • • • • • • • • •

Preheat the oven to 300 degrees.

Beat eggs together in a large bowl. Add milk and oil and beat well. Add dry ingredients; beat. Thin with more milk, if necessary, until mixture is the consistency of pancake batter.

Heat a little oil in a large skillet over medium-high heat, add ¼ cup batter and fry until bubbles appear all over the top of the cake. Turn and brown on the other side. Keep corn cakes warm in the oven while you cook remaining cakes.

Makes 12 corn cakes; serves 6.

Chili-Cheese Corn Bread

• •

PEOPLE IN THE RURAL SOUTH love to drink buttermilk. Most of the rest of us don't. But buttermilk has a long list of attributes, not the least of which is its flavor. It does great things for corn bread, biscuits, waffles and old-fashioned cakes.

1½	cups yellow cornmeal
½	cup all-purpose flour or whole wheat flour
1	tablespoon light brown or white sugar
1½	teaspoons baking powder
½	teaspoon baking soda
1	large egg, lightly beaten
1	cup buttermilk (you can substitute regular milk)
1	4-ounce can chopped mild green chilies, undrained
1	cup grated Cheddar cheese

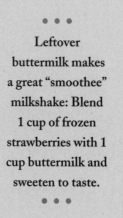

• • •

Leftover buttermilk makes a great "smoothee" milkshake: Blend 1 cup of frozen strawberries with 1 cup buttermilk and sweeten to taste.

• • •

Preheat the oven to 350 degrees. Butter an 8-inch square baking dish.

Combine dry ingredients in a large bowl. Stir to combine, smashing any lumps.

In a medium bowl, beat together egg, buttermilk, chilies and cheese. Stir briefly into flour mixture until just combined.

Pour into the baking dish and bake for 30 to 35 minutes, or until brown spots appear on top.

Makes one 8-inch corn bread; serves 6 to 8.

Fast Whole Wheat Rolls

• •

MOST PEOPLE NEVER MAKE YEAST BREAD because it's too intimidating and takes too long. But it tastes so good! These rolls are as easy as muffins and better for you: low in fat and full of nutritious whole grains. They have a crunchy exterior and soft insides and are made without the kneading, rising and overall angst that accompanies the preparation of conventional rolls. Go on: impress your friends!

1	cup whole wheat flour
1	cup all-purpose flour
6	tablespoons sugar
1½	teaspoons salt
1	package active dry yeast
1½	cups hot water

Preheat the oven to 350 degrees. Butter a muffin pan with 12 cups.

Combine flours, sugar, salt and yeast in a medium-size bowl. Pour in water and stir with 50 strong strokes to blend completely.

Spoon batter into muffin cups. Set aside for 20 minutes, or until dough has risen to the tops or a little above the muffin cups. Bake rolls for about 30 minutes, or until dark brown.

Makes 12 rolls.

English Muffin Bread

ENGLISH MUFFIN BREAD TAKES LONGER than most quick breads (the dough needs time to rise), but it's easier to execute than most yeast breads because it doesn't require kneading.

Like all bread, it's good fresh from the oven. It also makes great toast.

5 cups all-purpose flour (or substitute up to
2½ cups whole wheat flour, if desired)

2 packages active dry yeast

1 tablespoon sugar

2 teaspoons salt

2½ cups milk

¼ teaspoon baking soda, dissolved in
1 tablespoon warm water

This bread freezes well.

In a large mixing bowl, combine 3 cups flour with yeast, sugar and salt. Heat milk in a small saucepan or microwave on high power for 1½ minutes, until lukewarm. Add milk to flour mixture, beating well until smooth.

Stir in enough of the remaining 2 cups flour to make a stiff batter. Add baking soda-water mixture and beat again.

Grease two 8½-by-4½-inch bread pans. Divide batter between pans, cover loosely with plastic wrap and set aside to rise for 1 hour, or until nearly doubled.

About 20 minutes before baking, preheat the oven to 375 degrees. Bake for 1 hour, or until breads are browned and pull away from the sides of the pans. Turn out from the pans and cool on wire racks. Let cool a little before slicing.

Makes 2 loaves.

Mexican Pizza

• • • • • • • • • • • • • • •

Made with flour tortillas and Tex-Mex toppings, this could almost be a main dish, though it isn't as filling as traditional Italian pizza. I've seen these prepared by college students who consume them while standing up and reading the paper, but for a real meal, they'd probably be best served with soup or salad.

2 white flour tortillas

3 ounces Monterey Jack cheese, grated (¾ cup)

1-2 mild green chilies (from one 4-ounce can whole chilies), cut into strips

Chopped canned black olives to taste

Sliced scallions to taste

Preheat the broiler, with a rack 4 inches from the heat source. Place tortillas on the cookie sheet; broil 30 seconds or until tortillas just begin to brown. Turn and broil for 30 seconds more.

Sprinkle tortillas with cheese. Arrange chili strips and olives over the tops. Sprinkle with more cheese and then with scallions.

Heat under the broiler until cheese melts, about 30 seconds; watch carefully.

Serves 1. ∾ Serve with salsa.

Desserts

AHHHHH. . . SWEETS. Heavenly for dinner. Hellish for the rushed cook. Making dessert is like starting all over again. You've gotten dinner to the table, and they want you to bake?

But there are times when it's appropriate to provide sweets. When the grown-ups want the children to sit quietly for a few minutes. When the family's celebrating. When you're entertaining with a capital E.

For the cook in a hurry who needs to cope, fresh fruit is a simple but welcome dessert solution. In the winter, a mound of fresh tangerines can be dessert. Near my home, an orchardist grows hundreds of apple varieties in season from June until November. If I'm lucky enough to get some of his superior fruit, it alone satisfies. Similarly, when we've picked strawberries or lucked into good peaches or bought a seedless watermelon, the dessert problem is solved.

For times when you want more than fruit, good ice cream with homemade topping—a drizzle of liqueur or a sprinkling of candied ginger—is a please-all-the-people-all-the-time finale. And though ice cream can be served unadorned, it always seems a little more special with something on top.

Baking, however, is another story, requiring more time and more thought. My theory is this: perfect one or two or three recipes, and you'll have the repertoire you need to contribute to parties, school functions and dinners at home. Your desserts should ideally be portable, or you should have at least one that is. If you go to a Cub Scout meeting or a committee meeting, you can take the same dish. Variations on chocolate chip cookies always work, as do brownie and other bar variations. My almond pound cake can be altered to change the flavor, can be served in a variety of ways, can be baked ahead, can be frozen, and is so delicious it will appeal to everyone.

Remember that practice makes perfect. Toll House cookies seem easy because you've made them before, though the techniques aren't necessarily different from those of other baked goods. Anything you make once or twice will seem easier after that. Then when somebody says, "Please bring dessert," you'll know what to do.

desserts

Dried Fruit Compote

DRIED FRUIT COMPOTE is wonderfully easy and versatile. Make it for dessert one night and serve it with granola or yogurt the next morning for breakfast. It's a great choice during winter months, when most fresh fruits aren't in season.

The proportions given below are a guideline only. Depending on how dry your fruit is, or what type of mixture you use, you may need more liquid.

This recipe is best made with a fairly even mixture of several fruits. While the bulk of it can be apples, raisins and other inexpensive fruits, be sure to add some peaches, apricots and/or figs for interest.

¾-1 pound unsweetened dried fruit
     (raisins, figs, prunes, pears, apples)
     About 3 cups water
  ¼ cup honey
  1 2-inch stick cinnamon
  2 tablespoons orange juice concentrate
     (optional)

> • • •
> In place of water, try using herb or Earl Grey tea. Or substitute wine, port or Grand Marnier for orange juice concentrate.
> • • •

Combine dried fruit with water, honey and cinnamon stick in a medium-size saucepan. Bring to a boil, cover and simmer for 20 minutes.

Remove from heat, remove cinnamon stick and stir in orange juice concentrate, if using. Serve hot, warm or cold.

Serves 8 to 10. ∾ **Serve plain or topped with sweetened yogurt or as a sauce on pound cake, angel food cake or on French toast or waffles. Or serve with sour cream, custard, ice cream or whipped cream.**

Caramel Sauce

• • • • • • • • • • • • • • • •

THIS SAUCE IS for ice cream, pound cake, angel food cake, or anything on which chocolate sauce is usually served.

It's also for apple pie, or poached apples or pears, or other fruit desserts that go well with caramel. Nearly everything does.

> 1 cup sugar
> ¼ cup water
> 2 cups heavy cream
> 1 teaspoon vanilla or rum

Combine sugar and water in a deep medium-size saucepan and cook over medium heat, stirring to dissolve sugar. Raise the heat to medium-high to bring mixture to a boil. Use a metal spoon to scrape sugar off the sides of the pan; stir briefly.

When mixture darkens but is not yet as dark as brown sugar, remove from the heat and gradually add cream. (The mixture will splutter.) Return to the heat and cook, stirring, for about 5 minutes, until the mixture darkens and is the thickness of half-and-half; watch carefully and reduce heat, if necessary, to prevent spillovers.

Cool for 2 to 3 minutes and stir in vanilla or rum. Chill; the mixture will thicken considerably. Sauce may be served warm or cold; reheat over low heat.

Makes 2 cups.

Best-Ever Chocolate Sauce

• •

WHO SAYS YOU HAVE TO BAKE for hours to create wonderful desserts? The best possible chocolate sauce is also the easiest to make: two ingredients, a little heat, some stirring.

If you find that the mixture below is thicker than you need, you can add more liquid at any stage: some cream, evaporated milk or even plain milk. Don't substitute milk for cream in the recipe, though; you'll just end up having to add more chocolate.

> 2   cups heavy cream
> 12   ounces semisweet chocolate bits
>   (chips or chopped)

Bring cream to a boil in a medium-size heavy pot or in a large bowl in a microwave oven. Remove from the heat. Add chocolate bits and stir with a wire whisk until mixture is smooth, scraping the sides often. If chocolate has not melted completely, reheat very gently.

Cool to room temperature and use immediately, or cover with plastic wrap and chill. Covered well, this will last more than a week in the refrigerator and can be rewarmed. After that, it begins to turn grainy.

To rewarm: Place sauce in a microwave-safe glass or ceramic dish. Heat on low or medium power in the microwave for 30 seconds, stir and heat again until it reaches the proper consistency. Or rewarm sauce on the stove in the top of a double boiler or by placing it in a bowl and setting the bowl in a pan of warm water on low heat. Stir occasionally until blended.

Makes about 2 cups.

Almond Pound Cake

· ·

POUND CAKES and variations on pound cake make easy desserts. They freeze well, slice easily and are convenient to carry to bake sales or potlucks. This one is golden brown with a great texture.

1 cup (2 sticks) unsalted butter, softened
2 cups packed light brown sugar
4 large eggs
3 cups all-purpose flour
1 teaspoon baking soda
½ teaspoon baking powder
½ teaspoon salt
1 cup plain yogurt
1 teaspoon vanilla
1 teaspoon almond extract
   Powdered sugar for dusting

> · · ·
> Make Lemon Pound Cake by substituting lemon extract for almond.
> · · ·

Preheat the oven to 350 degrees. Butter and lightly flour the inside of a 10-inch tube pan or Bundt pan.

In a large bowl, blend butter and sugar with an electric mixer. Add eggs, one at a time, beating well after each addition.

Sift together flour, baking soda, baking powder and salt in a medium-size bowl. Add flour mixture to butter mixture alternately with yogurt; stir in vanilla and almond extract.

Pour batter into the pan and bake for 1 hour, or until a toothpick inserted in the cake comes out clean. Cool in the pan for 10 minutes; remove and cool completely on a rack. Dust with powdered sugar. Serve plain or with ice cream, chocolate sauce or fresh summer fruits.

Makes one 10-inch cake; serves 12.

Honey-Almond Ice Cream

• •

To MAKE A FAST, STRESS-FREE DESSERT after a special dinner, buy a good-quality ice cream and flavor it with liqueurs, chopped candy (Heath Bars or Snickers), or with honey and almonds.

¼ cup slivered almonds
1   quart good-quality vanilla ice cream
¼ cup honey

Preheat the oven to 350 degrees. Spread almonds on a dry cookie sheet and place them in the oven. Heat until they turn golden and smell toasty, about 5 to 10 minutes.

Divide vanilla ice cream among 4 goblets or ice-cream dishes. Place in the freezer until ready to serve.

Put honey in a heatproof dish and microwave for 10 seconds on high power or warm in a Pyrex custard dish set in a pan of water over low heat. Spoon honey over ice cream, dividing it evenly, and top with toasted almonds. Serve immediately.

Serves 4.

Fresh Strawberry Tart

· ·

THIS IS ONE OF THE BEST RECIPES for strawberry pie, slightly sweetened and served with cream. It features fresh strawberries, no red gelatinous goo. It's also the simplest. You don't think it's going to work, but it does. It slices beautifully. The recipe comes from Luckett Davidson, a Louisville restaurateur.

Tart Shell

1	cup all-purpose flour
½	teaspoon salt
⅓	cup vegetable shortening
2-3	tablespoons cold water

Filling

About ⅓ cup confectioners' sugar
About 4 cups fresh strawberries, halved or quartered, if large
1 cup whipping cream, beaten until thick

· · ·

This recipe may also be made with fresh peaches.

· · ·

To make tart shell: Combine flour and salt in a medium-size bowl. Using 2 knives, a pastry blender or your fingers, cut shortening into flour mixture until it is about the size of peas. Add water and blend with a fork until mixture holds together in a ball.

Roll out on a floured surface about ⅛ inch thick. Place in a 9-inch pie pan and trim any overhanging edges. (Pie crust may be frozen in the pie pan enclosed in a plastic bag at this point for up to 6 months.)

Preheat the oven to 400 degrees.

Just before baking, prick tart shell all over with a fork. Cut a piece of foil to fit the pan and brush with oil or spray lightly with a nonstick spray. Line tart shell with the foil, oiled side down, then weigh it down with beans, rice or metal pellets. Bake for 20 minutes, or until light brown. Remove the foil and cool tart shell.

To make filling: Sprinkle powdered sugar on the bottom of tart shell to make a layer about ⅛ inch deep. Fill with strawberries. Push down strawberries very gently; don't worry about filling every little space—just slight pressure will be fine.

Top with whipped cream, pressing down gently with a spoon so that it fills some of the spaces between strawberries. (It won't fill all the spaces.) Chill for 1 to 2 hours before slicing.

Serves 6 to 8.

Apple Crisp

· · · · · · · · · · ·

APPLE CRISP IS THE PERFECT APPLE DESSERT for people who loathe making pie crust. Some people even like it better than pie. A superior crisp combines several different types of apples: Granny Smiths, Galas, Golden Delicious and Braeburns or other cooking apples that mix tart, mellow and floral characteristics.

6 large apples, peeled and sliced (about 8 cups)
1 cup packed light brown sugar
1 cup all-purpose flour
¾ cup rolled oats
1 teaspoon ground cinnamon
½ teaspoon ground nutmeg
¼ teaspoon ground cloves (optional)
½ cup (1 stick) cold butter, cut into 6-8 pieces

Preheat the oven to 350 degrees. Butter a 2-quart casserole dish.

Place apples in the casserole dish. In a large bowl, with your fingers, combine remaining ingredients, rubbing butter in until mixture is crumbly. There should be no big chunks of butter.

Spread topping mixture over apples. Bake for 30 minutes, or until apples are tender and topping is golden brown.

Serves 8. ∾ Serve with cream, vanilla or caramel ice cream, custard sauce, sweetened yogurt, crème fraîche or caramel sauce.

desserts

Double-Chocolate Brownies

∙ ∙

BAR COOKIES ARE THE SIMPLEST kind of cookies to make and brownies are the simplest of bar cookies. I've done these in the morning before the shower and in between letting pets out, packing lunches and getting the kids to school. Grown-ups like the nutty version; kids usually don't.

4	ounces unsweetened chocolate
½	cup (1 stick) butter
4	large eggs
2	cups sugar
1	teaspoon vanilla
½	teaspoon salt
1	cup all-purpose flour
1	cup semisweet chocolate chips

> ∙ ∙ ∙
>
> For Double-Chocolate Nut Brownies, add 1 cup chopped pecans or walnuts with the chocolate chips.
>
> ∙ ∙ ∙

Grease a 9-by-13-inch baking dish with shortening or margarine.

Combine chocolate and butter in a small metal bowl and place over simmering water (or put it in a microwave-safe bowl and melt in the microwave). Stir occasionally until melted and remove from the heat; set aside.

Preheat the oven to 350 degrees.

In a large bowl, with an electric mixer, beat eggs. Add sugar and continue beating until mixture is lighter in color. Add vanilla and salt and beat to combine. Pour in cooled chocolate mixture and beat on low speed until mixed. Stir in flour, then chocolate chips.

Pour into the prepared pan and bake for 25 minutes; brownies should seem a little undercooked in the middle, still soft but not liquid.

Remove from the oven, let cool and slice into squares.

Makes about 2 dozen brownies.

Toffee Chip Cookies

· ·

FOR BUSY PEOPLE, there is rarely a good time to bake. But that doesn't slow down the requests: staff appreciation day at your school, fund-raisers, organizational meetings . . . Your contribution has to be recognizable, popular and easy.

Chocolate chip cookies are popular and easy, all right, but let's face it: they've been done. But if you vary the recipe by substituting toffee chips for chocolate chips, the results are gratifying. Toffee chips (called Almond Brickle Chips) are found in many supermarkets next to the chocolate chips. If you can't get them, use chopped Heath Bars. If you like, make giant cookies; they're quicker.

2½	cups all-purpose flour
1	teaspoon baking soda
½	teaspoon salt
1	cup (2 sticks) butter, softened slightly
¾	cup sugar
¾	cup packed light brown sugar
2	large eggs
1	teaspoon vanilla
1½	cups toffee chips (7.5 ounces) or five 1.4-ounce Heath Bars, coarsely chopped
1	cup chopped pecans (optional)

> • • •
> Overbeating the dough or overwarming the butter will result in flat cookies.
> • • •

Preheat the oven to 375 degrees.

In a small bowl, combine flour, baking soda and salt. In a large bowl, combine butter and sugars and beat until fluffy. Add eggs and vanilla and beat until creamy. Mix in flour mixture with a wooden spoon. Stir in toffee chips or Heath Bars and nuts, if using.

desserts

Drop by rounded teaspoons onto an ungreased cookie sheet. Bake for 8 to 10 minutes, or until browned on the edges and still slightly soft in the center.

Makes about 100 two-inch cookies.

Variations

To make giant cookies: Use a ¼-cup measure to dip in cookie dough. Press down lightly with the palm of your hand and bake for about 15 minutes. Makes about 20 cookies.

White Chocolate Macadamia Cookies: Replace toffee chips with 1½ to 2 cups chopped white chocolate or vanilla morsels. Replace pecans with 1 cup chopped macadamia nuts. (If macadamia nuts are salted, rinse them first under running water, drain well and dry by spreading them on a cookie sheet and placing them in a warm oven for a few minutes.)

Toffee Chip Bars: Spread dough in a greased 15-by-10-inch pan and bake for 20 minutes, or until edges just begin to pull away from the sides of the pan.

Index

Express Lane Cookbook